A guide to contact on separation and divorce

Fathers Matter

Celia Conrad

Creative Communications

Dedication

In memory of my beloved father
And for loving fathers everywhere

Published by Creative Communicat
Suite 530, 405 Kings Road, London

Production by Expression, IP23 8HF

© 2003 Celia Conrad

The law stated in this book is the law at July 2003. No liability is accepted for any errors or omissions.

ISBN 0 9546233 0 4

Further copies of this publication are obtainable from **www.fathersmatter.com**

Acknowledgments
I would like to thank all those fathers who, in speaking to me about their problems, have both encouraged and enabled me to write this book, but who perforce must remain nameless – they know who they are. Although it seems a long time since I was an undergraduate, I wish to thank my former law tutors at King's College, University of London, who taught me to analyse and question the law and not just to accept the status quo. Thanks to Tina and Stephen at Expression for their constructive ideas and speed of production; and to Tim at DoMedia for the website design. Finally, special thanks to my brother Stephen for his editorial skills and helpful comments.

Contents

Part II The law 54

Part III What does the future hold for fathers? 108

Preface

The idea for this book was conceived as long ago as 1999, while I was still working full time in private practice. One father, for whom my then firm was acting, asked me if I had considered writing a book to help address fathers' issues. After a chance encounter with a father in my local gym – my firm had ironically represented the mother – and to whom I subsequently spoke at length about his own predicament, I felt compelled to write this book.

The first draft was completed over two years ago at a time when, unfortunately, the whole issue of fathers' rights was still regarded by many as only a passing phase and I was told that there would be no interest in a book solely directed at fathers, as it would be too narrow and too controversial. This perception has persisted despite the fact that during this period of time there has been ever increasing media interest in the plight of fathers. Rarely a week has gone by without us reading or hearing about harrowing cases of fathers who have fought for but lost contact with their children, some of whom have been financially crippled in the process.

Frustrated by the lack of cohesion in this area and progress on their behalf, fathers' rights groups have been driven to take on the campaign for change themselves. This is no more evident than in the activities of Fathers4Justice, a civil rights group launched in December 2002 to support estranged fathers, which has gained enormous media coverage and aims to raise the public's awareness of the injustices fathers suffer and is pressing for change within the law.

The recent criticisms by fathers' rights groups of the judiciary, has sparked considerable debate. Are the courts biased towards fathers? Certainly, the majority of fathers who have been through the court process have no faith in it to produce an unbiased result. Their confidence in the legal system has already been undermined. A father is not interested in hearing his lawyer say to him at the end of a case, after he has expended thousands and thousands of pounds, that the result is very unfair and the legislation needs to be changed but there is nothing he can do about it because that is the law. This is not going to resolve the problem for the father and is regarded by many as 'a cop out' and does none other than to inflame an already heated situation.

I make no apologies therefore for the fact the content matter of this book may be regarded as controversial by some. The issues are controversial but they need to be addressed.

Introduction

The content of this book stemmed from a number of conversations I had with male clients during the course of their relationship break-up and in relation to their respective roles as fathers. Several clients told me that, on separating from their wives/partners, they searched the bookshelves in their public library and all the major bookstores in order to find some information for fathers going through a divorce, or who were 'splitting up' with their partner. The only guides they could find were for mothers.

Essentially what they were looking for was a user-friendly guide, which provided a thorough overview of the issues they now faced and addressed ways of dealing with those issues constructively. They indicated to me that they needed a comprehensive guide dealing with both the emotional impact on and legal implications of separation and divorce for fathers and their children. Although there were DIY divorce guides and books on child law, there were no specific guides relating to fathers' problems from a father's perspective. That is, to assist fathers with any queries, worries, and emotions – as well as the general confusion surrounding a divorce/ relationship breakdown. Additionally, they wanted to have a better understanding of their legal position and the legal process as applicable to them. In short they wanted a practical handbook for fathers.

I have written this book for all fathers who wish to build and/or maintain healthy relationships with their children after separation and divorce. I hope that by reading this book they will be able to cope better with the breakdown of their relationship and the adjustments that have to be made by them and their children upon separation. The breakdown of any relationship is traumatic and a degree of anger and conflict between parties is likely at this time. But when a relationship comes to an end, and especially in the early stages when emotions are riding high, understandably the parties often cannot see the bigger picture and the bearing that the actions of today will have upon their relations tomorrow, and the impact this will have upon their children because it is clouded by an emotional haze. It is evident that how parties interact, and what steps they take to reduce conflict and to resolve the issues between them, not only has a major bearing on their future relationship but also on their children and in turn that relationship. Both parents need to work together for the benefit of their children and to act in their children's best interests. This is crucial.

A father who has been able to reach an amicable agreement with the mother probably does not need to read this book. This book is directed at fathers who want to reach an agreement with the mother of their children but for one reason or another cannot do so. Clearly it is preferable, and ultimately in the interests of all parties concerned, to avoid court proceedings; but the reality is that for many a father reaching an agreement with the mother is like reaching for the moon. There may be some cases where all that is required is intervention from an independent third party to guide, direct and assist the parents, to enable them to work through the issues so as to enable them to forge an agreement acceptable to them. Both parents have to be fully committed to resolving the problem, and to finding a workable solution. But this is where the problems arise, as a lack of cohesion and compromise between the parties is generally one of the major stumbling blocks to reaching an agreement.

Independent third parties include counsellors, doctors, mediators and lawyers. Counsellors may be able to help with the emotional aspects; doctors with the symptoms of trauma and stress; mediators with clarification of the issues and assistance in putting them into perspective. A family lawyer has many hats. To a client on an emotional roller coaster, in the initial stages of a divorce or potentially heavily contested child application, a client may use their lawyer as a confidante, counsellor, emotional prop, punch bag, sounding board, listening post, psychologist as well as advisor.

Seeking the advice of a lawyer over a child issue does not mean proceedings must be commenced or at least not immediately – unless there is an imminent threat of danger to the child or the possibility that he/she might be abducted. In this situation court proceedings will be the first resort, on the basis that urgent action is required, since delay could be detrimental to the child. But if a father is in any doubt as to his legal position he should seek legal advice as knowledge of the legalities of a particular situation may assist in dealings with the mother. The role of a lawyer, as advisor, is to advise clearly and constructively so that rash decisions which a party might later come to regret when the consequences of those decisions come full circle are avoided. Unfortunately a complaint by many clients, male or female, is that it is the lawyers who all too often inflame the situation and are confrontational, aggressive, and litigious and add fuel to the flames. This in turn creates more conflict and is destructive.

The majority of fathers I have spoken to, who have taken legal action, told me that they did so reluctantly. The reality of the situation is that, although ideally they wanted to resolve questions relating to their children and avoid conflict, court applications and costs, they felt they had no other alternative as the contact arrangements proposed by the mother, or already in existence, were totally unacceptable to them. In some cases communication had broken down completely between the parties, or if they were still talking to each other they could not do so without arguing, and/or they were entrenched in their respective position.

Compared with the number of children involved, the number of cases that reach a final court hearing is small because the majority of cases are compromised along the way. However, this does not mean that fathers are satisfied with the compromise reached and that they are 'getting a fair deal' from the legal system. In fact most of the fathers I have dealt with did not think they had been well served and been 'squeezed' by it. A case might be compromised, for example, where a father wishes to protect his children from the 'fall out' of the proceedings and the adverse affect a court case may have on them, or where he gives up after receiving legal advice that his chances of success are next to nothing. Therefore the fact that a matter is compromised is definitely not an indication of a positive outcome for either the father or his children.

The Children Act 1989 assumes that the parties will do their best to resolve differences by negotiation and cooperation. It introduced a non-intervention and no-order policy. This means that the court will only intervene and make an order where it would be better to make an order than no order at all. This is ironic. The fact is the law only works for parents who are able to act in the best interests of their children and reach an amicable agreement, because in that situation the law does not need to intervene at all. The problem arises when parents cannot agree and the law is used to try to resolve what they cannot. Reliance upon the legal system to deliver what fathers want has left them bitterly disappointed. Unfortunately for a father, resorting to legal proceedings rarely achieves the desired result.

I did not write this book because I am pro fathers and anti mothers, but to highlight the areas of concern fathers expressly requested I address, to provide the information they need and to help raise their profile. In fact much of the material in this book is of relevance to both parents and not just fathers.

The book is divided into three parts. Part I deals with family matters, and the effect of separation on the family as a whole. We consider possible ways of resolving and/or reducing conflict between warring parents, look at contact issues and attempts to avoid court proceedings for the benefit of all parties concerned, particularly the children. There is a degree of overlap in relation to the issues raised in these Chapters, as familial relationships impact upon each other. Part II sets out the law. We examine the choice of lawyer, the law in context, the applications that can be made, the legal process and the court system. Finally in Part III, we review recent changes, and consider what the future holds for fathers in the light of some controversial case law, the vigorous campaigning by fathers' rights groups, proposed changes within the law and the recommendations made to improve this area of the law for the benefit of the children in the 2002 report *Making Contact Work*.

Part I Family matters

Chapter 1
The importance of fathers

A father's role

The concept of the family, and the role of a father within it, has been defined and redefined over the centuries. Traditionally it was expected and accepted that the male's role, as husband and father, was to go out to work and to provide financially for the family. The female's role, as wife and mother, was to run the home and care for the children and to be the emotional crutch of the family. By virtue of the fact that fathers were the breadwinners, and not at home with their children, their financial contribution was regarded as more important than their emotional one. A mother's relationship is 'seen' to be closer and it has been assumed that women, by nature, are better suited to love and care for the children.

How the family unit has changed

That 'traditional' concept of the family has completely changed. The stereotypical division of a mother and father's roles does not match the reality of the modern family. In today's society many parties do not marry, almost four out of ten children are born to cohabiting couples and there are more single mothers where no father is present at all. More and more women now have their own careers and therefore contribute financially to the family, sometimes equally or even more. There are also situations where fathers share the parenting duties with the mother, particularly where the father is self-employed and able to work around any child care arrangements. In fact, the father may even be the primary carer in a situation such as this.

The step-family is an ever increasing feature of modern family life where parties remarry. The National Statistics reveal that in 2000 the majority of stepfamilies (88%), in which there was at least one child from a previous marriage or relationship, consisted of a couple with at least one child from the female partner's previous relationship.

The definition of what constitutes a family is now very wide. Every case is different and generalizations should not be made about a father's role in this context.

The contribution a father has to make

What is a father's contribution to contemporary family life supposed to be? There has been a shift on the financial front so you might expect that this would mean a shift on the emotional front in favour of fathers. The reality is that from an emotional point of view mothers are regarded differently from fathers and there is definitely a lack of agreement about a father's potential role in child-rearing. Mother Nature is a major factor and the maternal bond is a very strong and special bond, but this does not mean that a father loves his child any less than a mother does or is incapable of loving his child as much.

There is no question that a father plays a crucial role in his children's lives, and they in his. In fact, in 1998 the Government produced a consultation paper *Supporting Families* in which it was stated that fathers do have a crucial role to play in their children's upbringing. Fathers have a very positive contribution to make to their families both emotionally and financially. This role is no less important than the one mothers play, albeit the role is played out differently. A mother and father each have a significant contribution to make. They have different styles of parenting and different attributes and should complement one another. Parenthood should be a partnership.

So to what extent does all of this impact on a father's role with his child after a relationship split? How does this affect his role?

Maintaining a role

Benefits for the children

The fact that a loving father no longer lives with his children does not make him any less significant, nor does it mean he wishes to be uninvolved with them. In the majority of cases this could not be further from the truth. A devoted father strives to have contact with his children and to retain a strong and positive presence in their lives. It is only circumstances that have dictated that he no longer lives with them. A father who does not live with his children is known as the 'non-resident' parent, a term which in itself is a bone of contention for fathers.

These fathers feel they provide the important function of 'being there' for their children. Many do this by helping with homework, attending parents' evenings at school and taking children to and from school. They can offer an alternative home when the need arises. They usually provide an important base for their children and relish taking responsibility for them, which they may not have had until they have sole care of them.

Certainly it is easier for a father to build a strong relationship with his children where there is a harmonious relationship between the parents, but that does not mean that a father who has to overcome obstacles cannot maintain a role although it is considerably harder.

What about cases where the father does not maintain a role?

Where does this leave the children of one parent families or where fathers do not wish to be involved? Are we to believe that these children will not be as well adjusted because they are denied that relationship? Many single parents will argue that this is not the case, and their children go on to do well at school and to form healthy relationships. Most of these children will have never known a father's presence. That may not be detrimental but it certainly does not mean that they would not have benefited from it.

It is of course a sad fact that not all fathers wish to have contact with their children. We hear reports from fathers of mothers who do their best to frustrate contact but there are many cases where, despite repeated pleadings from the mother for the father to visit, or even applications by the mother to the court for an order for him to have contact, the father still neglects his children. There are always two sides to every story and it is true to say that there are fathers who do not behave in a responsible manner.

There are cases where the father may have left his partner for someone else or just disappeared at the end of the relationship and ceased to have contact with his children. Then, after several years, he decides he wishes to re-establish contact and wonders why the mother does not play ball. It is no wonder that in these circumstances a mother protests and is hostile if a father turns up after several years demanding extensive contact and threatening her with court applications if she does not comply. On the other hand, for fathers who are consistent in their intentions and behave in a responsible manner towards their children there is no reason why contact should be denied. Cases of errant fathers must not be allowed to prejudice the cases of those fathers who are genuine.

We look in detail at fathers' post-separation relationship with their children in Chapter 4.

Fathers have feelings too

The emotional roller coaster

Fathers say that being separated from their children has a devastating effect on them. When they no longer see their children every day and/or their contact is limited or even prevented, they suffer a terrible sense of 'loss' and can feel helpless. Anyone who has lost someone very close to them only has to put themselves into a father's position and imagine his feelings in such circumstances. Men of course are not meant to be emotional – big men never cry. But they are and they do. Fathers are not immune to the emotional roller coaster. The emotions that emerge can come and go unpredictably, and they can feel up and then down and as if everything is out of control. They may experience feelings of grief, sadness, misery, desperation, desolation, isolation, rage, resentment, bitterness and hostility too. Sometimes the emotions are so overwhelming that fathers have suicidal thoughts. Sometimes they act on them.

I have seen fathers in a terrible emotional state and who have broken down in tears on the telephone, trying to come to terms with their situation. Numerous fathers have told me how heartbroken they were because they could not see their children every day. For fathers who are devoted to their children being separated from them is unbearable. A client who was a successful businessman said that the toughest decision he had ever had to make was in relation to his children. He felt emotional all the time but he was afraid of showing his true feelings because he believed it would be seen as a sign of weakness in the negotiations. It was no wonder that he was feeling emotional because he genuinely loved his children and was upset about the effect the divorce was having on them. The point is fathers have feelings too.

A father's predicament

Fathers find themselves in a no-win situation. They do not think the legal system addresses these points and that it has little regard for how they feel when decisions are made relating to their children. Right or wrong that is the perception. Unable to reach an agreement with the mother and faced with battling against the establishment it is no surprise that these fathers are under emotional stress. One father told me there were times when he felt like walking off the roof because he felt so desperate about his situation but the one thing which would always stop him taking that step was his love for his daughter.

A father often feels pushed right to the limit; desperate times may mean desperate measures. Some fathers take drastic action. Some fathers are so terrified of losing their children that they abduct them. While such action can never be condoned, there is a world of difference between a desperate father who just wants to spend time with his children and is driven to snatching them because he has not had any meaningful contact for months, and a father who abducts with malicious motive, who wants to punish the mother by taking her children away from her permanently and/or who poses a serious danger to the children.

There are some terrible cases where children have been abducted to a country with which the United Kingdom does not have a reciprocal agreement in respect of the abduction and return of children. These are known as non-convention countries as they do not comply with the Hague Convention which provides procedures for tracing children and their return. In any event, the consequences for a father who abducts are dire, because, if he is caught, he will have ruined any chances of meaningful contact with his child. This will be the case whatever the reason and ultimately it is the children who suffer the most. The issue of child abduction is addressed more fully in Chapter 13.

How fathers can help themselves

As matters progress, feelings change and the issues or challenges faced are also different. There are things a father can do to help himself make it through:

- Look after himself. It helps to cope with the changes going on around him. Eating and sleeping are important. At times of stress people do not/cannot/forget to eat and have difficulty sleeping.
- Keep focused on what the objectives are but be realistic.
- Take a step back and think about the implications of any actions taken and avoid making decisions that he will later regret. Revenge tactics may seem a good idea at the time but often backfire and do not bring about desired results.
- Talk about his problems to someone he can trust if he can. It does not change things but it may make him feel better because holding emotions inside can exacerbate stress and illness.
- Take time out for himself. With so many changes going on in his life at this time it is no wonder he probably feels overloaded.
- Consider writing down how he feels. Some fathers keep diaries to vent their frustrations.

One of the questions fathers ask is how they are meant to feel. There probably is no right answer. We are all individuals and one father may react differently from another. It also depends upon the particular circumstances. However, the range of emotions referred to above is indicative of a father's reaction in the majority of cases.

What about when matters become really bad?

It is common for people going through emotional trauma to feel depressed and have problems concentrating on work and focusing on anything else, because nothing else matters. Many fathers who run their own businesses report a major downward turn in productivity, as they cannot focus due to the surrounding uncertainty. They are unable to commit time to the business because they are devoting so much time to personal matters. Many fathers in employment find it difficult to hold down their jobs when their emotional life is in chaos. On the other hand, some fathers bury themselves in their work as a means of dealing with the fact that their family has fallen apart.

One father told me that he found it very difficult to cope when he could not see his children. He became an emotional wreck. He had been taking sleeping tablets and anti-depressants and became dependent on them. He developed severe depression and was withdrawn. Fortunately his family saw the warning signs and encouraged him to seek professional help. The support of his family and the qualified professionals helped him through. Others are not so lucky. They do not have that emotional support. Alone and depressed they become dependent on medications, other drugs or alcohol and unable to function without them. Sometimes it is all too much and the dreadful reality is that there are cases where fathers have committed suicide because they have not been allowed to see their children. The tragedy is that, on the face of it, these were fathers who appeared to be 'coping'. We do not hear of these cases though and this is an issue that must be addressed.

Help for fathers

There are an ever increasing number of organizations which provide information and support to fathers and actively campaign for fathers' rights. For any father encountering problems in relation to contact, or who needs general support and guidance, these organizations are well worth contacting because they offer a wealth of information for fathers. In the course of my research I have reviewed numerous websites directed at father-related matters, and this demonstrates how big this issue now is.

Chapter 2
Resolving issues amicably

Reducing conflict

How can parents resolve issues in relation to their children when they are at loggerheads? In the Introduction we looked briefly at how they deal with conflict and handle their relationship and why this has a major bearing on the way they resolve issues generally, including matters relating to their children. We now look at this more closely. We will look at the on-going parental relationship in Chapter 4.

The cycle of conflict

In any relationship each person is constantly reacting to the other. We may not think about this consciously but this is what happens. If someone is judgmental and critical towards a person how he/she reacts will be very different from how he/she reacts if someone is pleasant and full of praise for him/her. In the first instance he/she is more likely to respond well to the person, unless he/she has reason to suspect that there is a hidden agenda behind the display of warmth. Either way what is happening is that each person is determining the other's reaction. Put this in the divorce/relationship breakdown/contact context where there is an explosion of emotions, when parties are most likely to be feeling anger, hurt, guilt, regret, hate, fear and lash out at the other party. What happens then? It creates conflict.

How the cycle of conflict is compounded
Sometimes we feel that the only way to resolve something in our favour is to fight for it. If we fight enough we will achieve the desired result, so we believe, and the other party will back down. That may happen sometimes but generally what happens is the opposite. The more we fight someone the more of a threat we become to them and they fight back harder, and this in turn comes back on to us; there is a cycle of conflict. This is all too apparent in the father versus mother context.

Why fathers get caught up in this cycle of conflict
I asked a number of fathers why they fought so hard for contact. The answer was unequivocal: fear of losing the children. The problem that many fathers have is that on separation they are invariably the ones to

leave the family home so they immediately lose continuity of contact with their children. A father does not start on an equal footing with a mother. He is on the back foot.

If the child is an infant then the contact will generally be very limited, as he/she will stay with the mother unless the mother has a particularly good arrangement with the father and allows the child to stay with him. If the father moves into rented accommodation, it may be unsuitable for the children to stay there and other less satisfactory arrangements may have to be made.

Sometimes this means that a father will be unable to have as much contact as he would like with his children and, with relations in the family already strained as a result of the breakup, contact may be difficult. Fathers also fear about precedents for contact being set at these early stages. An agreement may not be possible and many fathers complain that they find it extremely difficult, next to impossible, to establish any regular pattern of contact with their children, so naturally they fight for it.

If fathers were guaranteed satisfactory contact then the fear of losing the children would evaporate and so would the need to fight for it. We know that court proceedings should be seen as a method of last resort. Ideally parties should look for an amicable solution. If court proceedings are issued they are generally resolved in some sort of compromise which nobody finds satisfactory; the final solution ordered by a court could even be less satisfactory. What are the alternatives for a father who has not seen his children for months due to the recalcitrance of the mother?

Breaking the cycle
In order to agree, parties need to communicate, but if communication breaks down and barriers go up that becomes a remote possibility, particularly when every attempt to communicate turns into an argument. The ideal scenario would be to take a step back from the other person and let matters calm down, not to enter into tit for tat arguments and focus on ending the conflict for the sake of the children. In reality, in such an emotionally charged situation where both parties are entrenched in their positions, the likelihood of achieving this is minimal.

Seeking assistance from third parties

Sometimes third party intervention can help but clearly it will not unless both parties are truly committed to the welfare of their children.

Counselling

Purpose

The purpose of counselling is to help the parties deal with the emotional side of their relationship. A party might attend counselling sessions for a number of reasons and those reasons vary from individual to individual.

Forms of counselling

There are different forms of counselling and different purposes for it. A father might want to find out if he can save his relationship and how he might do that. If his relationship cannot be saved then his purpose may be to help him cope with his feelings, and to come to terms with the situation. After separation he may seek counselling to help him deal with all the changes that are happening in his personal life. This includes the adjustments that have been enforced upon him in terms of his relationships with his ex, his children and any new partners on both sides. He may also want help in dealing with issues raised by other members of his family.

When people think of marriage guidance they think of Relate. Relate does not just provide Marriage Guidance Services but an extensive range of counselling services. It has offices in most areas. Organizations such as the Institute of Family Therapy, National Marriage Guidance, Jewish Marriage Council and Catholic Marriage Advisory Council provide counselling.

Mediation

Definition

If parties feel they cannot negotiate themselves but still wish to negotiate, then they can attend mediation sessions. Mediation is not Marriage Guidance. It is not counselling. Originally the mediation process in the UK was called conciliation but the word mediation is now universally used (probably because conciliation could be confused with reconciliation, and that is not what mediation is for). In mediation it is assumed the marriage has broken down and the focus is on helping the parties resolve the issues between them arising out of separation and this includes their children.

What the process involves

Mediation is a process open to a couple, married or unmarried, and the aim of it is to assist the parties to work though the issues between them with a view to reaching a compromise. It does not matter whether they are legally represented or not, nor whether they have started any legal proceedings. In mediation both parties agree to the appointment of a neutral third party who is impartial and who has no 'authority' to make any decisions in respect of their issues. In other words, unlike a court that will make a decision binding upon them, the mediator as a neutral individual is there to help them work through their problems. This is the case whether it is in relation to separation, divorce, children issues, property and finances or any other issues that may be raised. The mediator's role is to help the parties to reach their own informed decisions by negotiation and without adjudication.

In mediation the parties control the decision-making. The mediator cannot bind them to any decision, but is there to manage and control the process, guide them through the issues and will chair the meetings.

Can a mediator really help with children issues?

As well as dealing with 'all issues' mediation, there is also child-focused mediation. Mediation is a popular way to try and sort out contact problems. The mediators who work in this area may have experience as counsellors, social workers, family therapists or family solicitors.

If the mediation is child-focused the parties will concentrate on the children issues. They can discuss arrangements for the children, with whom they are to live, and how much time they should be spending with each parent, or whether they are to be looked after by another relative. A mediator can look at schooling and religion and encourage the parents to come to an agreement in relation to these points as well. It may well be that the parents are poles apart on these issues, and in particular on the 'living' arrangements for the children, but if nothing else a mediator might be able to help with interim arrangements.

Not a substitute for legal advice

Mediation may be a way of avoiding litigation but it is not a substitute for taking independent legal advice. Parties may want to take advice about what they discussed at the mediation. At the same time, there is no point in going along to mediation sessions if they do not go there with an open mind and are not prepared to tackle the issues between them. They will be wasting everybody's time including their own. If parties have legal advisors they should keep them fully informed of any progress made, as any legal action to be taken may depend upon the outcome of the mediation.

How much does mediation cost and how long does it take?

Mediation sessions are normally one and a half hours each. When giving advice solicitors generally charge by the hour, so if they are mediators they will generally charge their hourly rate. Some mediators operate a sliding scale of fees and the amount paid depends upon how much a party can afford, depending upon his/her income. There are some voluntary organizations as well. If a party has virtually no money at all he/she may be entitled to public funding through the Community Legal Service (CLS). CLS replaced the Legal Aid Board and has a scheme for funding mediation. (We look at the cost of funding legal costs and the role of the CLS in Chapter 7.) The number of sessions will depend on the issues, but five or six sessions are not uncommon.

How to find a good mediator

If parties are going to proceed with mediation then they need to find a properly qualified mediator otherwise they cannot hope to derive any benefit from it. This is essential as only a properly trained and accredited mediator can provide a quality and meaningful service for them.

To find a mediator a party could contact, among other organizations:

- The UK College of Family Mediators. This is the professional body for all family mediators in England, Scotland, Wales and Northern Ireland.
- National Family Mediation, NFM, is a registered charity and offers 'not for profit' family mediation services to couples in England and Wales. NFM is a Founder Body of the UK College of Family Mediators.
- The Solicitors Family Law Association's mediators are solicitors specializing in family law who have trained to be mediators. From January 2002 SFLA members who have been trained by other recognized bodies and have the necessary experience may apply to be SFLA mediators. They will have to attend a familiarization programme. As solicitors they have an in depth knowledge of the legal process and may be able to assist the parties to make fair and sensible arrangements both in relation to their finances and children. Alternatively, they may prefer an independent mediator totally removed from the legal process. At the end of the day it is up to the parties.
- The Law Society is the regulatory body, governing solicitors. It has produced a Family Mediation Code of Practice. The Code is addressed to solicitors who practise as mediators in family disputes. It has a specific section dealing with families and children.

Will the children have to attend mediation sessions?

The Law Society Family Mediation Code of Practice sets out specific guidelines for this. In all cases where children are involved the mediator should have regard to their needs and interests. The law provides that a mediator should have arrangements designed to ensure that both parents are encouraged to consider 'whether and to what extent each child could be given the opportunity to express his or her wishes in the mediation.'

The mediator should consider whether and when the children may be directly involved in mediation. The mediator should not ordinarily invite children to be directly involved unless specifically trained to do so and alive to issues such as confidentiality and the dynamics inherent in doing so. This is in accordance with the code.

It is extremely important that a mediator who wants to involve children in the mediation process should undertake specific training covering these issues.

Positive benefits of mediation

This is a 'conflict resolution' process, so in other words it is a means by which parties address and agree the issues between them and therefore avoid contested court proceedings. Even if they do not resolve all their issues, the fact that they have attempted to mediate is positive.

Mediation promotes co-operation between the parties, and looks at both their needs in the round rather than just one side, so compromise is more likely. Furthermore, it creates options other than winning and losing which is generally how parties will perceive their case once the court battle lines are drawn up.

Because each party has a say in the mediated agreement, it tends to include more specific details and actually reflects both their wishes, whereas if the matter proceeds to court there will be an enforced result and sometimes neither party will achieve what was set out for. A mediated agreement may subsequently form the basis of an agreed order to be submitted to the court, that is, a consent order.

However, the subject matter of any negotiations forming part of the mediation process is 'privileged from disclosure in subsequent court proceedings'. During the course of mediation sessions parties may discuss contact arrangements, but ultimately fail to come to an overall agreement and one party may decide to make an application to the court for a contact order. A party would not be able, within the context of those proceedings, to refer to what had been 'discussed' at the mediation sessions. This is the same in terms of any other negotiations that take place with a view to settlement, more commonly known as 'without prejudice negotiations'. This is important because if parties were afraid that anything they said could be used against them by the other party, they would never negotiate. Matters discussed in the mediation session are confidential except when a criminal offence is disclosed.

So this is a way of encouraging the parties to compromise and agree without putting them under pressure. It does not mean though that if parties do not manage to dot all the 'I's and cross all the 'T's at the mediation session that either of them should decide to change completely their position just to be awkward. It is not constructive, although it has been known to happen.

Clarification of legal position

If a father is divorcing or separating then it is likely he will be taking legal advice in relation to that as well as financial matters, and this will include maintenance for the children, where they are to live and their schooling. The children are likely to be at the forefront of any dealings with his solicitor.

Using the advice constructively

Ideally the advice given should be used to help resolve the issues with the mother. Focusing on finding solutions which are positive to everybody is the key to resolving issues without conflict. The difference between the parties resolving conflict themselves and an adversarial position, is that the former focuses on the need to find a solution and the latter on winning. At least that is how it is perceived. To the extent that they can do that, the legal process becomes redundant and costs are reduced. But again this is an ideal scenario and many parties never reach this stage because either or both of them simply have no intention of meeting the other half way.

We will look at the choice of solicitor in Part II.

Chapter 3
What about the children?

Telling the children

When parents separate and the father leaves, a child's world is turned completely upside down. Everything changes and the established pattern of life no longer exists. Children are faced with an abrupt change in their lives, especially so if their father suddenly leaves without warning and they had no idea that there were any problems at home. It affects their sense of security.

When, where and how

Children should be kept informed about what is happening between their parents as, after all, the changes are affecting them too and more than may be apparent. How, when and where they are told about the divorce and what they are told and understand can have a significant effect on their reaction. The way this is done can either reduce or increase their worries and fears.

All of this depends upon a number of factors including their age and understanding. How a child aged three is told that 'daddy has left' will be different from telling a child aged thirteen; all children are different. They will have views, issues and wishes too. The way they convey them will depend upon their age and understanding.

Timing is of the essence. Parents do not want to break the news to the children suddenly but they must not delay for too long either. If the decision to separate is final then parents must make that clear, because otherwise the children may pursue a false hope that their parents will be reunited. Parents should tell their children jointly if that is possible. The children need to be assured at all times that they are loved. They need to be told this on an ongoing basis and shown that they will be loved whatever happens.

The children may worry about any changes. Parents need to be specific and realistic about practical changes in their children's lives. They may be changing home, school, having to make new friends. If either parent has a new partner then they will have to deal with that new relationship too.

How the children might react

Relevant factors

It is very difficult to be exact about the impact of divorce/separation on a specific child although there has been much research into children's different reactions and there are a number of factors to consider:

- Their age and ability to understand, express and explain what they feel. Children's cognitive development varies.
- Gender. Girls react better than boys do apparently!
- Their nature.
- Their parents' relationship.
- Social background.

General reactions

Children may feel a terrible loss and miss the daily presence of their father in their life. They may convince themselves that 'this is not happening' and go into a state of denial. They may think that if they shut out the problem then it will simply go away. They may feel very angry and lash out at the father for leaving them, believing that he has betrayed them and has 'broken' up the family. They may become withdrawn and introvert. They may believe that they have in some way contributed to the 'break up' and feel it is their fault that their father has left because he no longer loves them as a result of something they have done.

When children realize that the situation is not going to change, despite anything they say or do, they can become very depressed. Parents need to look out for behavioural and emotional changes in their children at this time. Depression is apparently one of the most common psychological/psychiatric disorders and children are not immune, particularly when their parents separate. Feeling sad or depressed is a normal reaction to a tragedy, change or a significant loss.

General symptoms for children of all ages

These symptoms vary from child to child. Some may display many symptoms and others only one or two. Here are examples to look out for, some of which have been provided by former clients. Once again this list is not exhaustive:

- Crying, feeling sad, helpless or hopeless.
- Feeling discouraged or worthless.
- Loss of interest or pleasure in activities they used to enjoy.
- Bad temper, irritability.

- General lethargy, fatigue and loss of energy nearly every day.
- Fearful, tense, anxious, withdrawn.
- Drop in performance at school.
- Disruptive/destructive behaviour.
- Mood swings.
- Imagined illnesses where there is no medical cause.
- Appetite variations.
- Changes in sleeping habits.
- Bedwetting.
- Nightmares.

Reactions at different ages

The symptoms referred to above straddle the age groups and much depends upon the social environment and background from which the children come. If the parents are dysfunctional themselves, then the likelihood is that the children will be too.

If parents separate when children are babies or infants, the children will not remember a time when their father lived with them so they do not suffer the effects of the separation itself. There will not have been a change in their routine or life so far as they are aware. As we have seen when we looked at the father's role, the majority of fathers do not have the general day to day care of babies and very small children/toddlers because they are the breadwinners, so obviously the impact of the separation is not felt by these children in the same way as it is felt by the father. In these situations it is the father's ongoing role that becomes significant and more crucial. We touched on this in Chapter 1 and we look at this in depth in Chapter 4.

Small children between the age of about 5 and 10 are more likely to say they do not feel well or that they do not want to go to school. Their way of expressing they are not happy is by their actions rather than their words. They may become more aggressive and uncooperative or withdraw into themselves. For young children in particular there is a need for consistency in their lives and they are most seriously affected where it is lacking. The loss of daily contact with their father rocks their foundations. The security point again! Little children may not fully understand that their parents have stopped loving each other and, even if they do grasp that point, they may think that their parents will stop loving them too. Or, as we saw above, they may think that their father is leaving because he does not love them any more. They may become mistrustful.

Children between the age of 11 and 16 are very aware of discord, situations and atmospheres. They can feel guilty about parental conflict especially if they believe they are the source of the conflict between their parents. Older children may feel deep sadness and loss. Their schoolwork may suffer and behavioural problems are common. As teenagers they may experiment with drugs and/or alcohol and generally go off the rails. Teenagers may have trouble with their own relationships and experience problems with self-esteem that will follow them into their adult life.

How the parents' relationship impacts on the children's reaction

The effects of the relationship breakdown on the children are determined during the relationship and depend on the level of conflict between the parents. After a split, parenting and raising children may be more difficult. If there were conflicts or disagreements over parenting before the split, those problems will usually be worse and not better afterwards. Interestingly enough, the termination of a destructive relationship will probably be beneficial to the children because it removes them from an antagonistic and stressful environment. For these children this will be a welcome release from an adversarial and dysfunctional home life, and better for their psychological well-being.

What a father can do to help

We have looked at ways to resolve issues amicably in Chapter 2 and we will look at the post-separation relationship in Chapter 4. As indicated above, the parents' relationship has a direct bearing upon how they handle and react to the needs of their children. How skilfully parents can handle or mishandle their interactions with each other, and the children, makes a difference. Recognizing that children have a right to expect to continue to have the love and support of, and to enjoy a happy relationship with, both parents is very positive.

Put them first

A father can really help his children by letting them know that, whatever happens, he will always be fully committed to them and will love them, listen to them, and take account of their views. Because children tend to feel insecure at this time it is crucial to keep commitments and promises made to them. If a father cannot do that he must explain to them why not, otherwise they are left feeling that he does not really care even though that is just not the case at all. What an adult may not consider to be a big issue may be a major issue for a child. Children's reactions will be influenced by a father's ability to provide continuing emotional support and this sense of security. The children will fare best knowing that both parents remain involved with them, even though the family no longer lives together.

Be alert to signs of distress

It is necessary to be alert to any signs of distress that they portray and to look out for warning signals. By carefully observing his children, a father will see if they have anxieties and concerns and can give them the attention they need. If there is cause for concern it helps if a father can talk to the mother or at least agree that help from a qualified health professional – generally the GP in the first instance – could be beneficial.

Things a father should not do

Most of these points apply to both parents, not just fathers.

- After the parties have separated, and while they sort out all the arrangements, they should try to avoid the children being caught in the crossfire.
- Long legal wrangles or pressure for the children to 'choose sides' can be particularly harmful to them and can add to their distress. Children should not be faced with having to choose which parent is the better parent.
- Do not talk about the children within their earshot.
- Do not argue in front of the children.
- Do not manipulate, pressure or lie in order to make the children take sides.
- Do not use the children as messengers or spies.
- Do not exclude the children's involvement with the other members of the family, for example grandparents.
- Do not withhold information from the other parent.
- Do not speak negatively about the other parent. When children hear negative remarks about one of their parents they internalize it. This holds true for remarks concerning stepparents, grandparents and extended family members and any other significant person in the children's lives.
- This is not a time to use the children as a sounding board or an emotional prop.
- Do not make it difficult for the children to express their feelings. They need to vent them. Do not tell them how they should feel.

The children's wishes

A child's perspective

Children have a different perspective from adults. It should never be assumed that because the children do not talk about their concerns that they do not have any. However, they do like to be consulted and for their views to be heard. What are their views? Have these been taken on board? It is important to listen to what they have to say.

What are the children thinking?

A father needs to take into account what the children really want when making arrangements and talk to them, but remember that children often feel torn as they have divided loyalties and because they do not want to hurt their mother, or for their father to be cross with them, may sit on the fence. The children may have concerns and expectations regarding a father's new partner for example. Children may feel resentful of a new partner if they see her as the reason why their father moved out. They may think that he loves his new partner more than them.

Needs and requirements in light of age and understanding

It is necessary to look at what the children's needs are and consider what the difficulties are for them. It is very stressful for a child to see one or either or both his/her parents emotionally stressed. Children, even very small ones, are sensitive to atmospheres and pick up on when something is wrong. This in turn impacts on them and they are affected.

Where mature children are involved it is important to listen to their views. Their views may have an important influence on the terms of what is being discussed between the parents and the end result.

In any settlement where there are dependent children, their needs and welfare will need to be reflected in the terms of any agreement and, of course, in contested proceedings the child's welfare is the first consideration of the court and will be treated as paramount.

Stepchildren

The significance for them of the breakdown of the second relationship

In Chapter 1 we looked at how the family unit is changing. In Chapter 4 we look at remarriage and the introduction of a child to a new partner and potential stepparent. But what about the scenario whereby children have already been through the natural parents marriage breakdown, and one or both of the parents remarry and then one or both those second relationships fail? This scenario is, unfortunately, quite common because over half divorced parents marry again and sadly second marriages are more likely to fail than first ones, and therefore there will be many stepchildren affected by these breakdowns.

The breakdown of the first relationship is going to be bad enough for the children, but if there is a second split the children will go through trauma again, especially if they have become attached to the stepparent. In this situation a child's loyalties may have been torn between the natural parents and now they may be torn even further.

All the factors we have looked at above apply here as well.

Chapter 4
Post separation fatherhood

The post split father/child relationship

What is going to happen?

What happens to the father/child relationship after the parents' relationship breaks down? How does he maintain a meaningful relationship with his children? We have already talked about the importance of a father and his role. We touched on maintaining that role in Chapter 1. Many fathers say that, post split, their fathering role is never quite the same, but that they do manage to carve out a satisfactory role for themselves. For those who do achieve continuity in the fathering role there are, at the very least, transitional problems and glitches along the way. Very few indeed can achieve a completely smooth transition. Others report that they are unable to maintain a role at all.

Carving out a new role?

In the next chapter we look at how and why the father's relationship with the mother is so important for maintaining quality contact with the children. Sustaining an active and supporting role in the children's lives is weighted against a father if the inter-parental relationship is poor and this is the case no matter how much a father loves his children and wants to spend time with them. This is seen by a father as the biggest obstacle to contact and has serious implications for his relationship with his children. Fathers often have to jump through hoops in their attempts to fulfill a meaningful role.

Where inter-parental relationships work well, the father/child relationship generally does too. This does not mean that if the parents have problems then the father and his children will, just that it will be harder for a father to be involved and build the relationship he would like to have with his children. He will have to make a conscious effort to be a part of their lives and for fathers who do want to be a regular part of their children's lives it can be very tough.

Fathers feel that after the parties split there is always the danger that their relationship with their children will slide. Sometimes the battle against the mother for contact is too much and fathers give up fighting for it, or put up with severely reduced contact. To an outsider looking in, it may appear that the father has just walked away from his children because he simply does not care about them, and wants to shirk his responsibilities. The 'dead beat dads' as the media calls them.

Appearances can, of course, be deceptive. Fathers also state that one cause of major problems is the mother's new partner and the stepfather of their children. We look at this below.

Choices for fathers

Giving up

Into this category fall those fathers who have had to make extraneous efforts to maintain contact in a hostile climate. They may have had to deal with severely frustrated contact and/or court proceedings, but have still been unable to obtain any decent level of contact with their children. The emotional, physical and financial costs of continuing to pursue contact have taken their toll and they see their decision to abandon the fight as in the best interests of everyone, particularly their children. They argue that they are not opting out but making a sacrifice. These fathers do not wish for their children to be embroiled in bitter court proceedings and caught in the middle between their parents wrangling over them. Many of these fathers remain bitter and harbour resentment against the mother who they regard as vindictive and manipulative, and disillusioned with a legal system which they believe does not address the problems of being a non-resident parent.

Hanging in there

These fathers may have to face exactly the same problems as in the category above; they cannot communicate with the mother and face the same hostility. They are determined to keep the father/child relationship going by surmounting obstacles made by the mother so as to maintain a degree of contact with their children, if nothing else. They feel deeply unhappy with their situation, the continuing struggle, the enduring bitterness and conflict, and at times feel like giving up too. These fathers continue to maintain a presence, even if only a shadowy one, and take every opportunity to press for more contact if and when the occasion does arise.

Reinventing a role for father

Fathers say that the reality is that, being removed from the children for the bulk of the time, impacts upon their role as fathers. Understandably a 'two-day a fortnight father' feels he is losing out on the day to day routine of the children. Of course, this is a direct consequence of a father leaving the family home – which generally happens even if he did not initiate the separation – and for those fathers who did not want to separate in the first place this may be more of a tragedy. It is very difficult to recreate the same role in an abnormal situation where fathers are, in effect, stepping in and out of the children's lives. This is why children are often spoilt on contact visits, as the father tries to compensate for not being there all the time. Of course, this can backfire because the mother often says that the father disturbs the children's normal routine and equilibrium and therefore objects to contact. So this becomes a Catch 22 situation for the father.

Making the most of contact: pointers for fathers

Faced with the reality of limited contact, compared with the relationship that the father used to be able to enjoy with his children, is it any surprise fathers are tempted to spoil their children when they are with them on their contact visits or holidays?

Make contact as normal as possible

Clearly fathers want to treat their children, but it is when it turns into a competition between mother and father as to whose company the children enjoy most, that problems arise. A complaint mothers make is that fathers deliberately go out of their way to undermine them. They do this by spoiling the children, and giving them a better time than mothers are able to provide on a day to day basis. This causes resentment, although in the circumstances it is only to be expected that fathers may want to indulge their children when they do see them.

Keeping the children entertained

Fathers sometimes worry about what they should do on contact visits and how they are going to keep the children entertained. They worry that the children will be bored. When the parties were together they had a routine and probably the children were happy with that. Fathers might be surprised to find that their children are often just happy spending time with them. The problem here comes back to the fact that fathers want to make contact special because of the limited time they have to spend with their children.

Disciplining the children

When it comes to disciplining their children on contact visits, fathers generally tend to be more lenient. Fathers do not want to spend the time with their children disciplining them. One father told me that his little boy was very badly behaved on his Saturday contact visit, but he did not want to discipline him because that would probably have meant ruining the day, and so he let it pass as the time he had with him was very precious.

Avoid making any negative comments about their mother

Children sometimes repeat things that their mother may have said about their father which may not be altogether pleasant. It is better for the father to ignore the comment, or to deal with it casually, rather than to make a big issue out of it or respond with some vicious barb because, whatever she has said, she is still their mother. This works both ways. If a father has negative feelings towards the mother he should avoid directing them toward the children.

Be prepared to give a little

No agreement should ever be so carved in stone that it cannot be varied if necessity dictates. This applies even if there is a court order setting out the arrangements. Unfortunately, many parents rigidly adhere to these agreements, fearful that the slightest element of flexibility will weaken their position. It is a question of being flexible in response to a reasonable request.

Do not pressurize the children

Children need time to adjust to a change in their circumstances, different routines and unfamiliar surroundings. They now have two homes and in the initial stages moving between both parents' homes is emotionally trying. Parents need to think about how all this is affecting them. Children need to be surrounded by items with which they are familiar. They are more comfortable and relaxed knowing that they have their own possessions in both homes and that they will be there when they return.

Dealing with problems

Reasons for resisting contact

There are many reasons why children may resist contact. The most common reasons, with which many fathers are already familiar and that they may have to face, are as follows:

- They may not like his new girlfriend or wife or members of her family, particularly if she has children of her own. There may be stepsibling rivalry.
- The children reach an age when they have other commitments. They may want to go out with friends, they may have to study for exams,

have extra curricular school activities, and other interests that have become very important to them. Because they cannot spend so much time with their father this does not mean they no longer love him. It does not necessarily mean that they do not want to see him or that their mother is preventing them from seeing him. Fathers have to review contact arrangements and to reconsider their own role as the children grow older.

What to do if the children won't see their father

A father cannot force his children into wanting to spend time with him. This just makes matters worse. For example, if they do not like his new partner or they feel that he walked out on them, then the father has to take a step back and accept the situation. They may lash out at their father because they are hurting and he must not lash back. In time they may be able to rebuild their relationship with him. A father can often re-negotiate the relationship with his child but only when the child is ready. Sometimes he just has to be patient as with time they may accept the changes in his life; as they grow older they will have a better understanding of the situation. However, this is easier said than done.

Fathers feel rejected and insecure when their children do not want to see them. They think that their children do not love them any more and this hurts. They fear that they are losing their children. It does not help if a mother does not want to encourage the father's relationship. It may give her the excuse she has been looking for to reduce the contact. It is very difficult for a father to know what is best to do. All he can do is to make it clear he loves his children unconditionally and that he is there if they need him.

After this period of time has elapsed are fathers in a better position? Problems may ease in relation to the children once financial matters are resolved in a good many cases, but mothers do hold the trump card. You can tell a father that time will heal and when the children are a little older they can decide with their feet, but you try telling that to a father of a two-year-old child who is totally distraught that he cannot see his child. It might be a solution but it is hardly a satisfactory one.

External influences: dealing with new partners

Adjustments to be made

The break up may have been caused because one party has found a new partner. If not for that reason, they may have found someone since the split. They may decide to live together and subsequently marry. The new partner may have children of his/her own. Whatever the facts, a number of adjustments have to be made for both parents and the children. Sometimes the partner who has been left on their own can be very resentful of the other party's new found relationship and happiness, and problems bubble under the surface which can then manifest themselves in contact problems. The children themselves may have issues.

Introducing the children to a new girlfriend

One of the problems for a father with a new partner is introducing the children to her. When does he do this? What will they think? How will they react? He needs to be aware of his children's feelings. Loving parents will be concerned with any effect on the children. If the parties are arguing over contact and an application to the court has been made, the court will want to know whether the father is offering a stable environment since the court will not want the children exposed to different partners over a short period. Is the relationship stable? A father does not want to introduce his children to his new girlfriend, for them to become attached to her and then for her to suddenly disappear. This breeds insecurity.

Older children may be critical (or even jealous) of their father's new girlfriend. This is another example of where they may think that he does not love them any more, or as much, or be able to spend time with them. These are issues that will have to be dealt with.

Their mother may oppose the father introducing the children to his new girlfriend on the grounds that it is too soon, too disruptive and, even if initial contact takes place, she may firmly object to overnight contact taking place until the children have adjusted. She simply may not like his new partner. We look at reasons for a mother's opposition to contact in Chapter 4. This can cause a problem if prior to the father forming a new relationship he had overnight contact with the children. If the children react well to a new partner it makes it easier. If they do not like her, then there are problems.

The mother's new partner and its relevance to the father/children relationship

There is often resentment on the part of a father when the mother finds a new partner, they start living together and/or she remarries. A father's fear is not just that the new man might supplant him in the children's affections. The resentment often flows from the fact that the stepfather can see his stepchildren anytime he wants but the natural father can see his children only as agreed or by order of the court. That is a dire situation for a father to be in. It is intolerable.

Of course, a father can be deliberately awkward and if he wants to sabotage the mother's new relationship may use the children as pawns and oppose everything the mother wants to do, for example in relation to the children's schooling or medical treatment.

In one particular case the father was a bully and there had been physical violence to the mother during the marriage, which was why she divorced him. They had one child, a little boy. She remarried and had another child and her son developed a very good relationship with his stepfather. The natural father then began a major 'contact campaign'. He said that the mother was denying him contact, and not consulting him on issues relating to his son. The mother had not denied the father contact but the father took issue with the mother over everything relating to their son. She found it difficult to deal with him and if he did not agree with something he would threaten a court application, and then go and make it. This mother lived under the continual threat of the father making an application as soon as a contentious point arose between them. Instead of trying to resolve matters with her amicably, his solution was to make an immediate application to the court. On several occasions the first indication the mother had that there was a problem, was when she was notified of a forthcoming hearing in the post.

And another thing...

When parents remarry the mother/child bonds tend to be strengthened while the father/child ties are strained. Apparently, second wives are less likely to want to raise someone else's children, although there are many cases where both parties have children from previous marriages and it does not pose a problem at all.

Mother moving away

Generally, the further the distance between the children and the father, the harder it is for him to maintain contact with them and less likely that he can visit regularly. That is bad enough. Should a mother want to move to the other side of the world the situation becomes critical. For a father who has a regular pattern of contact with his children and/or has already had to surmount innumerable obstacles to ensure that he has a degree of contact, this is a nightmare scenario. Even where the mother is committed to contact with the father taking place, the reality is that no matter what her best intentions are, if she is on the other side of the world, at best that contact will be severely limited.

The welfare of the child is paramount, so is it in the children's best interest to see their father maybe a couple of times a year? How will the child be able to build a strong relationship with both parents? The move abroad prevents this from happening. Inevitably a father's contact would be severely reduced to holiday contact and he would therefore be denied involvement in the general upbringing of his child. Unless the father happens to be a millionaire, and most are not, he will not be able to afford to visit his children.

If a mother wishes to relocate out of the UK with the children and the father does not agree she must make an application to the Court for leave to remove them. We will look at this in Chapter 11.

Contact with the extended family

Grandparents

Contact subject to parental control
In the majority of cases when parties are together, the degree of contact that the children have with their grandparents will depend upon the parents because they control the contact. Should the parents not have a close relationship with the grandparents they will probably not promote the grandchild/grandparent relationship.

Post separation contact
After separation, the amount of contact children have with the grandparents is governed by the parent with whom the children live. Since this is invariably the mother, generally the maternal grandparents retain a closer link because they form part of her extended family to whom she will turn for support. Unless the mother has a good relationship with the paternal grandparents their relationship with the grandchildren will suffer. Grandparents can help the children because if they have supporting roles they can reduce the disruption of the parent's separation.

In one case the parties separated when their son was sixteen months old. The father remarried and moved far away. The mother had no alternative but to return to work full-time in order to make ends meet, so she entrusted the daily care of her son to her own parents since she could not afford child care. The maternal grandparents played a pivotal role in this child's upbringing. They cared for him every week day from 8am to 6pm until he went to school, and thereafter all the school holidays until he reached the age of fourteen.

Is promotion of contact generally dependent upon the mother or not?

A great deal depends upon the mother's relationship with the father's parents. Some mothers have amicable ongoing relationships with their in-laws and freely facilitate contact. In the case referred to above, the mother encouraged contact with the paternal grandparents, and she herself had an excellent relationship with the paternal grandmother. Unfortunately not all cases are like this and in many cases the paternal grandparents will be limited to contact when the father has contact visits – and even that could be severely curtailed if the mother raises objections.

Additionally, if it was the mother who had previously encouraged contact with the father's parents and no longer does so, then the split will be detrimental to the paternal grandparent/grandchild relationship. Thus the loss/lack of contact with paternal grandparents might occur not because the mother prevents it, but because the father leaves the responsibility for maintaining contact with her, even though they are now apart.

Other family members

Children can feel torn when there are a number of other relatives pressing for contact. Usually children will have more contact with the relatives of the parent with whom they live. Contact may become more fragmented when parents remarry and step relations are introduced.

Parents see their relatives as important sources of support and turn to them in times of crisis. They may also be dependent on their family for emotional and financial support and this can be ongoing and sometimes that puts a strain on those relationships too. Given the heavy reliance on the extended family during this period, it is difficult to imagine how a father who does not have an extended family copes alone at this time.

Chapter 5
Friend or foe: dealing with your ex

Working together

Acting in the children's best interests...

Parents must try to avoid settling old scores by using their children as pawns. They need to cooperate and support each other for the sake of the children, keep the lines of communication open and put their children first. Even though they no longer live together in the same household, fathers will always be fathers and they and their children need quality and quantity time together. They are ex-husbands and partners but not ex-fathers!

Facilitating contact

Mothers need to facilitate contact and encourage their children's relationships with their father. There will always be exceptions. For example, where a father has abused, neglected or deserted a child, or where there has been domestic violence and the mother opposes contact, what is in the best interests of the child will be something the Court will have to decide. We look at a mother's justification for preventing contact further below. How the Court deals with these issues is addressed in Part II.

In cases where both parties are genuinely acting in their children's best interests, and the problems in the above paragraph do not apply, they may find some way to sort out the contact arrangements. In previous chapters we have talked about avoiding conflict and agreeing arrangements but we have not looked at the arrangements themselves.

Contact schedules

Parties may work out a contact schedule and agree dates for contact, where that contact will take place, how long the contact visits will be, including collection and return times. They should consider the arrangements for staying contact and holiday contact. Will the children stay overnight? What are the holiday plans? What is feasible? If the children have a routine, that will need to be factored into the arrangements. Do the children have extra-curricular activities? Can contact arrangements be made to fit around them?

Both parties have to expect that very occasionally arrangements need to be altered. Although last minute changes should be avoided, sometimes this cannot be helped due to some unforeseen event. For fathers who travel abroad on business, agreeing a rigid contact schedule in advance can be very difficult because it is not always possible to schedule business arrangements and trips around contact. Sometimes business plans are changed at the last minute too and are not within the father's control. Flexibility is required on the part of both parties if contact arrangements are to work well.

The parental relationship

Although the parties' relationship has come to an end, their parental relationship is ongoing. They need to work on that relationship together as parents for the sake of the children. Conflict between parents makes contact very difficult. Probably the most accurate test as to whether the parties have adjusted after their split is to look at the level of conflict between them. It is not a good sign if parents are constantly at each other's throats and it is certainly not healthy for children to be caught in the crossfire.

The goal of everybody, advisors included, should be to reduce conflict between former partners thereby reducing the negative impact on the children.

Parental Interaction

A father's relationship with the mother is highly significant when it comes to his ongoing relationship with his children. Fathers confirm that the 'type' of relationship they have with the mother has a direct bearing upon the quality of contact they enjoy with their children, and that the majority of disputes arise from ongoing or recurring conflict.

Relationships between former partners fall into a number of categories. They may have a relatively positive relationship and can separate out their issues, enabling each parent to have a quality relationship with their children. They may be amicable or able to tolerate each other for the benefit of the children. In this way the 'emotional' disruption of the break up is reduced. On the other hand, they may have a very negative relationship where conflict has a nasty habit of breaking out at the slightest sign of tension between the parties, and where there is a lack of support, cooperation and trust. This causes 'emotional' stress for everybody involved.

What type of relationship do the parties have?

Friends

Parties may fall into this category because for one reason or another they have decided to separate, but the decision is mutual and often based on the best interests of the children. They may have just drifted apart and although they may not 'love' each other any more, still like and respect one another and recognize that each parent has a valid contribution to make to the children so they work together.

If one party does have any negative feelings towards the other, he/she does not let those feelings interfere with the parental relationship. Because they put the children's welfare above their own they have workable and flexible child arrangements and emotional disruption to the children is minimized. This type of relationship is not very commonplace and more parties fall into the next category.

Formal acquaintances

If parties fall into this category then they will probably be less at ease with each other and child arrangements will therefore be on a more formal footing. There may be conflict between them in relation to their own issues, but they manage it and do not allow this to spill over into their relationship with the children. So, although they will not be friends, they will make compromises for the sake of the children and make agreements in their best interests which still have the necessary flexibility to work well. Both parties will make joint decisions over important matters relating to the children and exercise their parental responsibilities well. This relationship allows the children to maintain a healthy relationship with both parents.

Warring parties

If parties fall into this category then there will be a lot of anger, bitterness and resentment in their own relationship which has not been dealt with which spills over into the parental relationship. They will find it very difficult to separate out and discuss child issues and argue over the smallest points always re-opening old wounds when they try to negotiate.

Their relationship is strained and, even if they can come to some form of agreement regarding the children, there is little flexibility in the arrangements. This means that contact will be difficult and the children will be caught up in the midst of it all and have torn loyalties. Members of each party's respective families may become involved in the squabbles and the children will be affected by the poor relationship.

Sworn enemies

If parties fall into this category their own relationship problems dominate and they cannot communicate on child issues. They see each other as enemies and dwell on all the negative aspects of their relationship and lose focus. There is a great deal of anger for one reason or another and it is not dealt with so matters do not improve. Since they cannot agree child arrangements, they invariably resort to court proceedings to battle it out, and this in turn causes more conflict. The contact is constantly frustrated and they enter a vicious circle of conflict.

Everybody is affected and children become pawns. Every opportunity is used to score points against each other. A father in these situations often fights harder for contact in the initial stages, but over a period of time may gradually withdraw to reduce and/or avoid conflict because he cannot continue with a full scale war for various reasons. In such circumstances the father and children both suffer.

Disconnected partnerships

Into this category fall those relationships where, after the parties split, the father moves away completely and all contact is discontinued. The father generally withdraws from his former partner's life.

Parents may start off in one category and move into another. Many couples start off in the warring parties' category and then move into the formal acquaintances' category. This may be due to time healing matters between them or because they have made the conscious effort to improve their relationship for the sake of the children. Open communication between parents is the key. It is important for each parent to continue to communicate with the other no matter how they feel.

Communicate to negotiate

It takes two...

It cannot be emphasized enough that in order to resolve matters both parties need to communicate. Each party will have views and want those views heard, but the way those views are communicated to the other party can make a difference. So how can they communicate constructively and productively?

Communicating effectively

The common ground between the parties should be to find a solution that is in the best interests of their children. If they keep that goal in sight, then they will both attempt to communicate. Neither party can force the other to communicate nor to make an agreement, but for a father there are things he should bear in mind if he plans to try and resolve child issues with the mother. He needs to:

- Be clear about the issues he wants to discuss and think about areas of potential conflict.
- Decide where he is going to meet the mother. Think about a neutral location.
- Start off with issues that are not in dispute.
- Think about the children's wishes. Has he talked to them and asked them what they want?
- Listen to what the mother has to say and explain why he holds a particular view on a certain issue.
- Be prepared that there are things he may need time to consider and not feel that he has to give an immediate response and also be prepared to compromise. Maybe neither party has considered all the options. Give and take is important in these situations.
- Decide what his boundaries are. How far is he prepared to negotiate? What is negotiable and what is not?
- Keep reminding himself that he is communicating to resolve matters amicably in his children's best interests not his.

Maternal gatekeeping

As we have seen, where the parents own relationship is poor then problems with contact are compounded. In such circumstances fathers are faced with a dilemma. They want to see their children but are often thwarted. Fathers mention situations where the mother prevented contact with the children, and the health, safety or wishes of the children had nothing to do with the refusal!

Sabotaging the father/child relationship

When fathers leave the family home and there is conflict, one of their concerns is that they are going to be dependent upon the mother to facilitate contact and to promote the father-child relationship. Fathers refer to mothers actively trying to sabotage their relationship with their children and trying to 'poison' the children against them in order to destroy a previously loving relationship.

In the United States this is known as Parental Alienation Syndrome. This is where mothers attempt to programme the children and use psychological tactics to destroy the relationship! Nothing is ever so clear cut. There are a number of factors to consider including the strength of the father/child bond in the first place, the ages of the children, what the children might actually decide they want for themselves and external influences such as the mother's new partner.

What do fathers consider to be sabotage?

Sabotage does not just relate to the contact visits, but the whole father/child relationship. Mothers may try to exclude fathers from issues relating to the children and in effect sideline or in drastic cases oust them from their lives altogether. The following list is not exhaustive but it includes common complaints made by fathers against mothers:

- The mother calls the father at the last minute to change the contact arrangements or to cancel the visit by which time the father is probably on his way.
- The father arrives to pick up his children to be told that they are ill.
- The father arrives to pick up his children and there is nobody at home.
- The father calls to speak to his children and the mother either makes an excuse for him not to speak to them, says they are out, busy or refuses to allow him to speak to them.
- The children do not receive the cards and presents that the father sends through the post because the mother withholds them.
- The mother does not inform the father about medical, schooling and other important matters and constantly tries to make important decisions about the children without consulting the father. For example, when the father does not attend a parents' evening or school event, about which the mother has failed to inform him, she then tells everyone that he cannot be bothered and is not interested in the children.
- The mother encourages the children to regard her new partner as their father.
- The mother says that the father is irresponsible and that he does not care for the children properly when they are with him.
- The mother blames the father if the children are badly behaved saying that it is his contact visits that disturb them.
- The mother says the father tries to undermine her relationship with the children on their contact visits!

Sabotage by mother or justifiable position?

Although from a father's perspective a mother may appear to be sabotaging contact, this may not be her intention at all. Some mothers may genuinely believe they are acting in the best interests of their children, even if it is an ill-founded belief and without any justification whatsoever. Fathers would argue that many mothers are being deliberately obstructive as a means of exacting revenge on them. Unfortunately, this is true in a number of cases, but there are situations where a mother has real cause for concern; matters are often neither black nor white but a variable shade of grey.

Examples of reasons for maternal sabotage provided by fathers
The following list is not exhaustive:

- The mother regards the father as a bad lot. He is not worthy to be the father of her children. Even though the parental relationship has failed this should not adversely impact on the father's relationship with his children. One father told me that he felt very guilty that he could not make his wife happy and he was totally responsible for the breakup of their marriage, but that she was now trying to punish him by being as awkward as possible when it came to contact.
- The parties may be caught up in an acrimonious financial battle, and a complaint sometimes made by fathers is that some mothers use contact as a tool to engineer a better financial settlement. By the same token, mothers sometimes claim that fathers put financial pressure on them as a means to force them to agree to more generous contact. Power struggles ensue...
- The mother may really hate the father. If he was the one to break up the relationship or walked out on the family she may use the children to exact her revenge on him. Alternatively, she may still want to be with the father and cannot accept that the relationship is over and uses the children to exert some pressure.
- The mother has found a new life for herself and does not want the father to be part of it. She sees his intervention as bothersome and no longer desires to be in touch with him and wants to cut him off.
- The children may be all the mother has, she has become emotionally dependent on them, and is possessive of their love and jealous of their relationship with the father and fearful that in some way he might take them away from her.
- The mother feels resentful towards the father's 'generosity' to the children on contact visits, feeling she cannot compete.
- The father may have a new partner; she resents her, neither likes her nor wants her as a rival for the children's affections, so finds reasons why the children cannot have contact with their father.
- The mother may have a new partner and she wants to establish her new family unit and for the children to think of him as their father.

A mother's justifiable concerns
Some examples:

- When the parties initially separate everybody involved is disrupted, especially the children. There are many adjustments that need to be made. A mother may argue at this time that if the children have weekend staying contact with their father this will cause disruption and that it will take her several days to re-establish their routine therefore overnight contact is out of the question. Fathers complain about this, but the fact is this is often true. The problem for fathers is where this is an ongoing issue, even after a period of time, when both parties have settled into their new routines and homes.

- The father may have remarried or have a new partner and there are problems over introducing the children to her and when staying contact may be appropriate. There are various factors to consider. The children may react well to the situation or they may not, and do not want to stay overnight anymore. Mothers report children being very distressed and bedwetting. Fathers see this as an excuse for avoiding contact.

- The mother may have genuine concerns about the welfare of the child. She may have reason to believe that the father is not looking after the children properly on contact visits. They may return from contact visits dirty, or with only half the clothes she sent them with, and they may not have been fed properly.

- In a situation where a father has set up home, not with another woman but with another man and the mother is worried about the environment in which the child will be placed.

- Where there has been domestic violence.

- Where there has been abuse/maltreatment or the mother suspects it.

- Where the mother has other reasons to believe that the children are or might be in danger. Examples of this would be where the father was an alcoholic or drug addict or was mentally unstable.

A final word ...
Many mothers go to extreme lengths to ensure their children have flourishing relationships with their fathers and try to separate their own relationship from the parental one. These mothers actively support fathers' desires to stay involved with their families. By all accounts contact is an extremely sensitive and emotive issue and striking a balance is very difficult because each parent may have a different agenda and view of what is in the best interests of the children. Each case has its own specific set of circumstances, but one thing is certain: a child has two parents for a reason and should have every opportunity to build a loving relationship with both of them.

Part II The law

Chapter 6
In brief: the law and legal system

The law in outline

The Children Act 1989

This Act is the principal statute dealing with children. The Act was introduced to simplify the law relating to children and to consolidate and unify the court system. When the Act came into force in October 1991 most of the existing children legislation was repealed.

The Act is divided into two parts: the first part relates to private law and the second part to public law. Under the Act private law means the law between individuals, for example parents, and relates to their rights over, responsibilities towards and proceedings in respect of children. Public law means the law relating to the responsibilities and proceedings in respect of children where public bodies are concerned. This covers local authority care cases.

Private law orders
There are five main types of private law order that the court can make under the Children Act and which are of interest to fathers, as follows:
- Parental responsibility order. The Children Act introduced a new concept of parental responsibility. Essentially what parental responsibility means is having the responsibility for taking all the important decisions in a child's life on a day to day basis. We look at parental responsibility in detail in Chapter 8.

The four other orders are known collectively as s8 orders:
- A residence order: If a party has a residence order this means their child will live with them.
- A contact order: If a party has a contact order (usually the father) this requires the person who has residence (usually the mother) to allow the

child to visit or stay with the father or for other forms of contact to take place such as telephone calls, letters etc. We look at the different forms of contact in Chapter 12.

- Prohibited steps order: A father would apply for this order to prevent the mother taking a particular step without the prior consent of the court. It is an order for forbidding actions.
- Specific issue order: A father would apply for this order where he has, or may have, a disagreement about a specific question in connection with any aspect of parental responsibility for his child and he needs the court to direct how it will be resolved. It is an order permitting actions to take place.

Public law orders
It is not within the ambit of this book to deal with public law save where local authority proceedings impact upon a father's contact with his child. We will look at this briefly in Chapter 12.

Underlying principles under the Children Act
When the court makes any order under the Children Act relating to the upbringing of a child it will consider:

- The child's welfare. This shall be the paramount consideration of the court. There are a number of factors the court will review and these are known as the 'welfare checklist'. See below and Chapter 10.
- Whether to make 'no order'. Where the court is considering whether or not to make one or more orders under the Act, it may decide not to make an order or any orders unless it considers that making an order would be better for the child than making no order at all. The Act assumes that parties will endeavour to make their own agreements. In other words, it has to be in the best interests of the child to make an order. This is known as the non-intervention principle.
- There must be 'no delay'. The court will want to deal with matters as quickly as possible. For a child several months is a long time. Delay could be detrimental. This is why the court regulates the timing of cases.

How the court decides

The court will have regard to seven factors when considering the welfare of the child:

- The ascertainable wishes and feelings of the child concerned, considered in the light of the child's age and understanding.
- The child's physical, emotional and educational needs.
- The likely effect on the child of any change of circumstances.
- The age, sex, background and any characteristics of the child which the court considers relevant.

- Any harm which the child is suffering or which the child is at risk of suffering.
- How capable each of the parents, and any other person in relation to whom the court considers the question to be relevant, is of meeting the child's needs.
- The range of powers available to the court under this Act in the proceedings in question.

Each of these factors is referred to in detail in Chapter 10.

The courts and court protocol

The courts

In private law matters, proceedings can be commenced in any court that has jurisdiction to deal with the case. The courts that deal with children matters in the first instance are the:
- Magistrates Court (Family Proceedings Court).
- County Court.
- High Court.

Which is the right court for the case?
The Magistrates Court does not deal with divorce. If there are divorce proceedings these will be filed in the County Court and an application under the Children Act will be made there within those proceedings. An unmarried father would make what is known as a free-standing application under the Children Act and he might start proceedings in either the Magistrates Court or the County Court.

The judges in the County Court are known as District Judges and hear private law family work. The Principal Registry in London is a Divorce County Court. The High Court can hear all types of Children Act applications. It will generally deal with the more complex cases, which could either be started there, or those which are transferred up to it from the other courts. For example, a case transferred up from the County Court. Cases can be transferred down as well. It depends on the circumstances. The Children Act introduced a unified court system to make transfers between courts easier.

Court layout and dress
Family proceedings are more informal than other legal proceedings and generally held in chambers, which means they are in private and not open to members of the public (unlike criminal proceedings). In these

circumstances neither the judges nor the advocates wear gowns or wigs. The layout of the court varies from court to court. Usually the seating arrangements are more relaxed and the court is often a large room with the Judge sitting at the head of a table and the parties and their advisors on either side.

The Principal Registry is in High Holborn, London. It deals specifically with family cases. In these courts the District Judge sits on a raised platform, there is a witness box and there are several rows with seating for the parties and their advocates. The Family Division of the High Court is based in London at the High Courts of Justice in the Strand. These courts are similar to the courts at the Principal Registry but much larger and less modern than the former.

There are instances where family proceedings are held in open court, which means the press and members of the public are allowed into court. Of particular relevance to fathers are committal proceedings for contempt of court orders. For example, where a mother refuses to hand over a child for contact and is hostile and repeatedly in breach of Court orders, there is provision to apply for her to be committed to prison. This is rare and is explored in more detail in Chapter 13.

Relevant court personnel

- Counter clerks. These form part of the administrative personnel. They are not legally qualified and therefore do not give legal advice. They have various roles but specifically there are clerks who deal with the issuing of applications, lodging of court forms, payment of court fees and listing of cases.
- Court clerks, Associates and Ushers. When parties and their advisors arrive at court they need to inform court staff that they are present. The court needs to know who is in attendance and the names of the parties and their representatives. In the County Court the Clerk will be allocated to a District Judge. Any papers that the Judge needs to review before the hearing must be handed to his clerk. The clerk will be present in court, and generally sits below and just in front or to the side of the District Judge. The clerks have a number of duties: they pass papers to the District Judge when they are handed up from the parties or their advisors, swear parties in if they are to give evidence, liaise with the listing office over hearing dates and draw up court orders made by the District Judge further to the hearing. They are not legally qualified. In the High Court the usher wears a black gown and literally ushers parties in and out of court. The associate's role is essentially the same as the court clerk.

Court address

How should the Judges be addressed?

- Magistrates are referred to as: Your worship, sir or madam.
- Deputy/District Judges as: Sir/Madam.
- County Court Judges as: Your Honour.
- High Court/Court of Appeal Judges as: My Lord (M'Lord), My Lady (M'Lady).
- How are solicitors and barristers addressed in court?
- The Judge will refer to them as Mr... or Mrs... or Miss... as appropriate.
- Solicitors refer to fellow solicitors as: My friend, Mr ... Mrs...or Miss as appropriate.
- Barristers tend to refer to each other as: My (learned) friend, Counsel for X.

The role of solicitors and barristers

Both solicitors and barristers may appear in court on behalf of their clients in child cases. Solicitors provide ongoing legal advice to the client and deal with the day to day running, management and preparation of a case. They are responsible for the preparation of court bundles which generally contain the following documents: all the court applications, orders made by the court, statements of the parties, child and family reporter's report, experts' reports and relevant correspondence as applicable to the particular case. They attend court hearings, either presenting the case themselves or attending as instructing solicitor with the barrister they have retained to present the case. The decision by a solicitor to appear at court depends upon the complexity of the case and the issues involved.

Generally, and there always exceptions, solicitors deal with early direction appointments and less contested applications in the court process. They are more inclined to instruct a barrister as the case progresses because the barrister is a specialist advocate. Barristers will be instructed to advise on the issues and briefed to appear on behalf of the client at court and present the case. There are Juniors and Leaders. A party has a Conference with Counsel and a Consultation with Leading Counsel, known as QCs, that is Queen's Counsel.

In children's proceedings an atmosphere of negotiation and cooperation between professionals is encouraged. They are supposed to be non-adversarial. Unfortunately, the very nature of the legal system encourages the opposite.

The court process

The basic procedure in children's cases is the same. The court application and process is addressed in Chapter 10. Here we deal briefly with general procedure at every hearing.

General procedure

The person who makes the application is known as the Applicant and the person against whom the application is made is known as the Respondent. At each hearing the applicant's advocate introduces the other advocate and the parties to the court. The parties stand while the Judge enters the court, nod and remain standing until the Judge sits.

The length of the hearing will vary depending upon the issues involved and the stage of the case. The case will be allocated a time in the court list – but sometimes cases overrun and there can be a considerable waiting period, particularly in the High Court.

If a parent has legal representation and does not attend at court it will not prevent the hearing proceeding, unless it is necessary for that particular parent to give evidence or an order has been made for the parent's attendance by the court itself. There are occasions where it is possible to obtain an order without the other party being notified and present at court. These are known as ex parte orders and we look at these in Chapters 10 and 13.

The courts are extremely cautious where a party is not represented by a solicitor and fails to attend a hearing. A party representing themselves is known as a litigant in person. The court will ask the other side to provide documentary evidence that this party has been properly served with the proceedings and is aware of the hearing date. This involves producing a statement of service and/or sworn statement from process servers to prove that the party has been properly notified of the court hearing. If the court feels that there has been proper service of the papers then an order may be made. Sometimes hearings are adjourned to a later date; for example, due to the non-attendance of a party because of illness. The circumstances of the case and the nature of the hearing will have a direct bearing upon the decision made by the court.

Unless it is a final hearing, or an interim hearing where the parties are to give evidence and are to be cross-examined (in other words where there are witnesses) it will be a case of the applicant's advocate opening the case and outlining it to the court. Then the other parties' advocate has the opportunity to make a speech to the court. A judge may ask further questions and there may be some interaction between each party's advocate and the judge to assist the judge in making their decision. The judges will then make the order.

At a final hearing the applicant's advocate opens the case and calls all the witnesses in support of the applicant's case and questions them on their evidence – that is the witness statements they have filed at court setting out their case and which have been served on the other party. This is known as examination in chief. The respondent's advocate has the opportunity to cross-examine those witnesses. The Family Court Reporter, formerly Court Welfare Officer, is invariably present and may be questioned. Once the applicant has presented the evidence it is the turn of the respondent and all of the respondent's witnesses to give evidence. The applicant can then cross-examine those witnesses. The judge will then give judgment. Sometimes judgment is reserved while the judge considers the issues.

What is CAFCASS?

This is the Children and Family Court Advisory and Support Service. It has been operational since 1 April 2001 and combines the services which, until then, provided advice and recommendations to the courts about children and their families, one of which was the Family Court Welfare Service.

Court Welfare Officers were responsible for the preparation of reports in child cases. They were important as the welfare report carries weight in court. Fathers in particular raised concerns that many Family Court Welfare Officers did not have a social work qualification and that they spent little or insufficient time with a child and his or her family to assess the situation adequately. There was a lot of criticism because of this and because the report has such a major bearing on a case fathers have been up in arms about it.

The majority of staff transferring into the new service possess a social work qualification. As indicated, Court Welfare Officers are now termed Family Court Reporters and I am advised by CAFCASS that 99% have a diploma in social work.

The purpose of the service is to assist the courts to make decisions that are in the best interests of the children affected by family proceedings. Since its evolution it has been criticized for not being as effective as it should be and recommendations have been made to make it more so. In February 2003 the House of Commons Select Committee began an enquiry into CAFCASS and the Report was published on 23 July 2003. Included in the findings were that the service lacked adequate funding, had insufficient staff and that there needs to be provision for proper training of staff, professional development and performance management.

Chapter 7
Your solicitor

How do I find a good family solicitor?

It is very important to find a solicitor who is a specialist family practitioner and therefore fully up to speed with family law. There are tales of clients who have been given poor legal advice by a solicitor who is not a family law specialist and who have lost out as a result. The choice of solicitor is important because the way a case is conducted can have a major bearing on the outcome. There are many firms that have strong family law departments with specialists who can draw on each other's strengths and have the expertise to deal with all aspects of family law.

Personal recommendation

Most family solicitors obtain new clients through the referral process; either through former clients or business associates such as other solicitors, bankers, accountants and financial advisors. Personal recommendation from friends who have divorced recently or had problems over family issues such as contact is very common. It is worth asking friends which firm of solicitors they instructed and in particular who dealt with their case, why they instructed that firm and the quality of service that was provided. So far as quality of service is concerned, this covers not only the advice given but also how they were treated generally.

Reputation

A father might decide to instruct a firm of solicitors because he has heard they have an excellent reputation for family law or he wishes to instruct a particular solicitor because he has heard about his/her personal reputation. It depends upon the approach he is looking for. A hard-hitting lawyer specializing in family finance may not be suitable for children proceedings. It is all a question of balance. At the end of the day, he needs to have confidence in his solicitor and the solicitor needs to instill confidence into him.

Law Society

The Law Society is the regulatory body for solicitors. They will be able to assist a father in finding a family specialist in his area. If he wants to find out more information about a solicitor, that is, whether they are a Partner and how many years they have been qualified, the Law Society will be able to provide this information.

Solicitors Family Law Association

The Solicitors Family Law Association's (SFLA) members are solicitors who are all family law specialists. The SFLA has a Code of Practice for its members to adhere to. A copy may be obtained by contacting the SFLA. Solicitors who are members of the SFLA should endeavour to advise, negotiate and deal with issues constructively and quickly with a view to encouraging a settlement and try to avoid conflict. In children's cases the approach is to be conciliatory and the aim is to deal with the issues in a non-confrontational manner.

Where children are involved the SFLA code directs family solicitors to see their work as most important and to act accordingly.

Memberships

The Solicitor may be an Accredited Specialist on the Law Society Family Panel or Children Panel or an SFLA accredited Family law specialist. A solicitor may be a lawyer/mediator as well.

Other considerations which may affect the choice of solicitor

How much they cost

Solicitors charge on an hourly basis, and their hourly rate will depend upon how senior they are and where they are based. It is important to find out how much that hourly rate is before the first meeting. Where funds are limited a party may be entitled to a contribution towards their costs. This used to be called Legal Aid. The Legal Services Commission (LSC) has now replaced the Legal Aid Board. Not all firms undertake LSC funded services so that is something to clarify initially.

Solicitors charge for all time spent on a file. This is called chargeable time. This includes telephone calls made to the solicitor by a client and calls they make to the client or to third parties in relation to the case. All correspondence received and sent out is charged for, including e-mails and faxes. A client will be charged for meetings, perusal of documents, analysis of documents, preparation of documents, conferences with the barrister, attendance at court, travel time to and from court and conferences, and the travel costs.

Case management

If there are a number of solicitors in a firm who specialize in family law it is important to find out if there will be anyone else working on the file and what their charge out rate is. It may well be that the Partner instructed may delegate the case to a more junior member of staff, such as an Assistant, to deal with on a day to day basis. The Partner will continue to oversee the file and the Assistant will keep the Partner informed and refer to the Partner on important matters. From the client's point of view this has two implications:

- There is another point of contact and this is very useful if the Partner is often unavailable, in court, on holiday or ill, and
- This should reduce the costs.

Sometimes clients are not very happy about a more junior member of staff dealing with their case because the whole reason why they may have instructed a firm in the first place is that they want a particular solicitor to act for them. The reality is that Partners with busy practices will have to delegate work to a junior member of staff because they cannot handle all the work themselves and it is not cost effective for them to do so. However, Partners who manage their practices well will not delegate work to a more junior member of staff who is incapable of dealing with it. They will inform the client, and explain why they are delegating the matter and that they will oversee the file. They should also introduce their Assistant to the client at the earliest opportunity.

If clients have any concerns about the quality of work or the advice they are receiving they should feel able to raise them. Clients should never feel that they cannot question the progress of their case. The client is paying for the advice received and if there are queries about who is dealing with the work, or any of the work being undertaken, it should be questioned sooner rather than later in order that any problems can be addressed and rectified.

Personal qualities to look out for

Family solicitors have different styles. Feeling confident and comfortable with the solicitor instructed is crucial.

Affability

Obviously the solicitor/client relationship is a professional one, but the very nature of the work makes it much more 'personal' as family clients have to provide solicitors with intimate details of their lives. Therefore it is very important for a family client to be able to relate well to his/her solicitor and to build up a rapport with him/her. A client wants and needs a solicitor who is approachable, not gruff and standoffish. Clients like to feel that they can trust their solicitors implicitly and that they are patient, sympathetic and empathetic but also constructive, objective and polite, but firm when needs be.

Availability
The nature of family work is such that the solicitor will have a very hectic schedule and cannot always be there at the very instant a client calls. He/she may be on the 'phone or in a meeting or at court. If a client leaves repeated messages and calls are not returned then he needs to find out if the messages have been passed on or where his solicitor is and why he has not received a response. A solicitor's secretary can be of invaluable assistance to a client. It is important to build up a good rapport with the secretary because at the very least she will be able take an accurate message in her boss's absence and she may be able to deal with the query. Obviously she cannot give legal advice, but she will be familiar with the file so is a very good point of contact.

Ability
Clients also need someone who is in command of the subject and can advise thoroughly on their case, who has a grasp of all the issues and who can instill confidence and, of course, who acts constructively.

Characteristics to avoid

Arrogance
Solicitors who denigrate other solicitors to boost themselves are unprofessional because they inflame the situation between the parties. In family cases this is particularly detrimental and can do a great deal of damage. Confrontational solicitors will turn the process into a battle because they like to win. The whole case is in danger of turning into a battle of egos between the parties and their solicitors because this unconstructive behaviour promotes conflict.

Aggression
Sometimes family lawyers have to be very tough to fight their client's corner, but a party cannot negotiate if his/her solicitor turns every issue into a battle. Being tactical is a completely different point. Negotiation requires skill and is time consuming but is likely to be far more productive than aggressive correspondence.

Antagonism
A father should watch out for actions backfiring. He has to live with the

consequences of any legal action taken long after his solicitor closes the file. If the solicitor makes his job more difficult then he should consider instructing a different solicitor.

The solicitor/client relationship

Giving and receiving advice

Instructing the solicitor
It is for the client to instruct the solicitor and for the solicitor to advise the client. The client should listen to the advice, but if he is dissatisfied with all or part of it and feels unhappy about pursuing a course of action proposed then he should make his instructions understood and not be forced into taking any action with which he is uncomfortable. If he has doubts about the advice he should take a second opinion.

Seeking clarification
If anything is unclear the solicitor should be asked to explain, otherwise the client may find himself going down a path he never intended. The solicitor will advise on the facts provided by the client, so a client needs to tell the solicitor everything to enable him/her to advise properly. Sometimes a solicitor will only be able to give initial advice, if full details of the case have not been provided.

Help to keep the costs down
In order to keep costs down, the client should try to be as organized as possible and be clear about what he wants to discuss with the solicitor before making the call or attending the meeting. By producing any information/documents requested as quickly as he can and dealing with any queries his solicitor raises promptly, he should be able to cut down his costs.

Terms of business and costs

The costs letter

The Law Society requires all solicitors to inform clients in writing about their terms of business. The terms of business letter or letter of engagement will set out details of the solicitors who will be dealing with the case and how much their hourly charge out rates are. A solicitor has a duty to keep a client informed as to the level of costs and of any changes in the charge out rates so that the client is fully aware of his costs position at all times. If the matter is likely to proceed to a contested hearing, the solicitor should provide the client with an estimate of costs and include the barrister's costs in that estimate.

Payment of costs

The client is responsible for payment of his solicitor's bills for the work carried out on his behalf. A bill should include a summary of the work undertaken. It will set out the solicitor's costs and stipulate the period of time these costs cover. The solicitor's costs are profit costs and disbursements. Profit costs mean all the chargeable time spent on the file during the period of the invoice and are subject to VAT. Disbursements are the other expenses the solicitor has incurred on the client's behalf. Some disbursements are subject to VAT such as counsel's fees, telephone, postage and copying. Some disbursements do not attract VAT including court fees and oath fees.

Costs queries

Bills are to be paid within 30 days of an invoice otherwise interest becomes payable. A client can request a breakdown of the bill and if he wants to challenge a bill he may do so. The back of the invoice will explain what to do if he does not accept the bill.

Different considerations apply as to whether the case involved court proceedings or not. If not and the bill has not been paid, within one month a client could ask his solicitor to apply for what is known as a Remuneration Certificate from the Law Society.

This is a certificate stating that in the opinion of the Law Society the sum charged is fair and reasonable or, as the case may be, what other sum would be fair and reasonable. As well as applying within one month of the bill, a client will have to pay half his costs, VAT and all the expenses. Alternatively, he can write to his solicitor saying that he will pay the whole bill on condition that they obtain a Remuneration Certificate and if this is unacceptable they will have to return the payment. If there have been court proceedings then he could ask for a detailed assessment of his costs. If he is confused about how to proceed he should contact the Law Society and/or Supreme Court Taxing Office. The Office of Supervision of Solicitors at the Law Society will be able to provide helpful guidance.

When a party instructs a solicitor to act for him it is known as the 'solicitor/client retainer' but he can terminate the retainer by giving written instructions to his solicitor at any time. The solicitor can terminate the retainer only with good reason and on giving reasonable notice. Until a client's costs are paid the solicitor is entitled to retain the file of papers. This is known as a 'lien' on the file.

The terms of business letter should set out whom a client should contact in the event of a complaint.

Public funding

If a client is funding the case himself, he is a private client, but if a client cannot afford to fund his costs he may be entitled to public funding. Legal Services Commission (LSC) funded services are only provided by solicitors who have a contract with the LSC. For family work the contract must actually cover the specific type of case. A client will need to give full details of his finances to his solicitor for them to assess his financial eligibility. He has to show that his capital AND income are within the current financial limits and these change on an annual basis. Any funding certificate may be limited in terms of the work the solicitor can undertake, and the amount of costs that can be incurred. What is available in family proceedings?

Approved family help

This covers assistance in resolving a dispute through negotiation or otherwise, including issuing proceedings and representation where necessary to obtain disclosure of information from another party, or to obtain a consent order following an agreement of matters that were in dispute. It covers cases up to the full representation stage so it covers the final court hearing. There are two forms available:

- Help with Mediation. This is limited to giving legal advice and assistance to support family mediation. This is only available if a party is taking part in Family Mediation or has successfully reached an agreement or settlement as a result of Family Mediation.
- General Family Help. This is for legal advice and assistance on family matters and to cover negotiations where a party is not attending mediation. Generally it will not be granted unless the suitability of the case for mediation has been considered.

Legal representation

This level of service is so that a party can be represented in court if he is taking or defending court proceedings. This is the same level of service previously called Legal Aid. There are two forms available:

- Investigative help. The funding is limited to investigating the strength of a claim.
- Full representation. The funding is provided to represent a party in legal proceedings.

  A certificate will not be backdated, but in some cases involving children the solicitor can act immediately. If a case is urgent the solicitor may be able to apply for emergency Legal Representation.

With Legal Representation a party may have to pay a contribution depending upon his financial status and this will be calculated for him. Contributions from income are by way of monthly instalments but contributions from capital have to be paid as soon as he accepts the offer of a certificate.

In terms of the costs a party pays, if he wins this depends on whether the other side is ordered to pay his costs and in fact does so. If he loses, then the most he will normally have to pay towards his solicitor and barrister's costs is his contribution under his certificate. The court will not normally order him to pay his opponent's costs but it may do depending upon his conduct and will be dependent upon his own financial position.

Chapter 8
Getting to grips with the basics

I am the natural father so I must have rights?

Just because a man is the natural, that is biological, father it does not mean that he has. It depends on the circumstances.

Married fathers

If a man was married to the child's mother when the child was born then there is a presumption that he is the father of the child, and this is so even if by the time the child is born the parties are divorced.

Unmarried fathers

If a man was not married to the child's mother there is no such presumption. What about registration of the birth? Does this confirm rights on him? If his name is on the birth certificate that may be evidence of paternity, that he is the father, but it does not automatically provide him with parental responsibility. The Adoption & Children Act 2002 amends the Children Act and provides that the biological unmarried father who registers his children's birth jointly with the mother will obtain parental responsibility. However, the new Act will not be retrospective, so a father who registers before the new Act is in force will not be able to rely on the provisions. The provisions are being phased in gradually with full implementation planned for 2004.

Parental responsibility

Meaning

The Children Act defines this as 'all the rights, duties, powers, responsibilities and authority which by law a parent of a child has in relation to the child and his property'.

It means having the responsibility for taking all the important decisions in the children's lives relating to their day to day care, religion, education, and medical care. The emphasis is on 'responsibilities' towards the children and not rights over them. Parental responsibility is to be exercised for the benefit of the child not the parent. The duties involved in parental responsibility will change from time to time depending upon the age and maturity of the child.

Does the father have parental responsibility already?

If the father was married to the child's mother at the time of the birth then he will have parental responsibility automatically. Married parents both have 'joint' parental responsibility. Any person with parental responsibility may act alone and does not have to consult anyone else with parental responsibility, but common sense dictates that where both parents have parental responsibility they should consult with each other and not take important steps unilaterally. So far as unmarried fathers are concerned, the amendments to the Children Act by the Adoption & Children Act will enable more of them to acquire parental responsibility; but not all unmarried fathers will be covered under the new law therefore it is necessary to consider the other ways to acquire it.

Is parental responsibility necessary?

For a father, parental responsibility enables him to be involved in the day to day decision making relating to his children so for an unmarried father who does not acquire it automatically, and who wants to be involved, this is a big issue. For example, without it he may have difficulty obtaining information about his children from their school or doctor. For an unmarried father, who lived with the mother and was involved in the day to day care and decision making relating to their child, it can be a rude awakening to find that without parental responsibility he is not in a position to question the upbringing of his child!

Acquiring parental responsibility

For an unmarried father who has registered his children's birth prior to the implementation of the new provisions, he can still acquire parental responsibility as follows:

- By entering into a parental responsibility agreement with the mother. This must be on a prescribed court form. An agreement may be terminated by order of the court either on an application of a person with parental responsibility, or with leave of the court, on an application by a child with sufficient understanding.
- By applying to the court for a parental responsibility order. We saw in Chapter 6 that this is one of the five main private law orders made under the Children Act. The court will look at the degree of commitment which he has shown towards his child; the degree of attachment which he has shown and which exists between him and his child; and his reasons for

applying for the order. If he satisfies the test, the presumption is that a parental responsibility order should be made. Where a father has shown himself willing and anxious to pick up the responsibility of fatherhood, then the law should give him parental responsibility.

- By being appointed a guardian either by the mother or the court. Note, however, that he will assume parental responsibility only in the event of the mother's death.
- By obtaining a residence order from the court. This automatically gives him parental responsibility. We will look at residence applications later.
- By marrying the mother.

Can an unmarried father without parental responsibility automatically apply for a s8 order?

He can because, as the natural father, he has an automatic right to apply to the Court.

Can a father apply for a parental responsibility order where his child was not born in the UK and does not reside here?

Irrespective of whether the child is resident here or was not born in the UK, it is possible to obtain a parental responsibility order.

Can a father lose parental responsibility?

He will not lose it due to someone else obtaining it. This is because, as indicated above, more than one person is allowed to have parental responsibility. In fact, there is no limit to the number of people who may have parental responsibility at any one time.

But he can lose parental responsibility in the following circumstances:

- The natural father will lose it on death or if his child is adopted. Adoption automatically extinguishes parental responsibility.
- An unmarried father who obtained a parental responsibility order could lose it if the court makes an order ending it. For example, if he inflicted serious injury on his child.
- A stepfather who acquired parental responsibility by being granted a residence order will lose it automatically when the residence order terminates. In fact, anyone other than an unmarried father will lose it in these circumstances.

What happens if the father entrusts his children to the care of someone else?

It is not possible to transfer or surrender parental responsibility, but the father can delegate responsibility for a child on a temporary basis. For example, this could be to a school for a school trip or to a nanny or child minder. Temporary carers do not acquire parental responsibility, but may do what is reasonable while the child is in their care for the purpose of safeguarding or promoting the child's welfare. This includes a stepfather who does not have parental responsibility. For example, this could cover emergency medical treatment.

When does parental responsibility come to an end?

Parental responsibility will come to an end as regards any issue in relation to a child's upbringing as soon as the child itself is mature enough to make a decision about that issue. A balance needs to be struck between parental responsibility on the one hand and the wishes of a mature child (having listened to that child's views) on the other.

In terms of children being able to take responsibility for their own actions, it depends what it is they want to do and their age and understanding and therefore this will vary from child to child. The law prescribes certain ages where it deems that the child will have reached a certain level of maturity to do certain things. For example, at the age of 16 a child could:

- Leave school. If a child attains the age of 16 years during the period from 1 September to 31 January, the child may leave school at the end of the spring term following his sixteenth birthday. In any other case the child may leave school on the Friday before the last Monday in May.
- Marry with parental consent or a guardian's consent or that of the court.
- Endorse his/her consent on a deed poll to evidence a change of name.
- Consent to sexual intercourse.
- Consent to surgical, medical or dental treatment.
- Be sold cigarettes and tobacco.
- Ride a motor bike.

At the age of 18 children reach the 'age of majority' and are fully-fledged adults and capable of making their own decisions – unless they are mentally handicapped and incapable of making their own decisions, in which case different considerations will apply.

Stepfathers

The relevance of stepfathers and parental responsibility

There may be a situation where the mother has children from a previous relationship and remarries. Her new husband treats the children as his. They are children of the family. However, marrying the mother does not automatically give a stepfather parental responsibility, unlike the natural father.

What are the ways a stepfather can acquire parental responsibility?

Presently he can do this in three ways:
- By being appointed guardian to care for the child if the natural parent dies;
- By obtaining a residence order stating that the child lives with him. If he is married to the child's mother and the child has been living with him for 3 years or more, or he has the consent of everyone with parental responsibility, he has a right to apply for an order. However, it is unlikely that the natural father would consent.
- By adopting the child.

Limitations

As set out above, if a stepfather obtains a residence order then he will only have parental responsibility for as long as that order is in force. Parental responsibility does not give a stepfather the right to consent – or refuse to consent – to the making of adoption orders in respect of the child, or the right to remove the child from the jurisdiction. In all other respects, he will have the same parental responsibility for the child as the natural father.

Changes

The Adoption & Children Act has amended the Children Act to insert a new section in respect of the acquisition of parental responsibility by stepparents. This provides that a stepfather will be able to acquire parental responsibility in other ways as follows:
- If he is married to the mother, and she agrees to him having parental responsibility, provided the natural father also agrees (where he has parental responsibility), he can then enter into a parental responsibility agreement.
- He can make an application to the court himself as a stepparent for a parental responsibility order.

Further Changes

There is also a scenario where one of the partners in a single sex relationship already has children and the other partner plays a significant role in those children's upbringing. In the Consultation paper on Civil Partnerships (July 2003) it is proposed that where there is a registered partnership, a registered partner should be able to obtain parental responsibility in the same way as a stepparent to enable them to have a full part in the children's upbringing.

To clarify, a civil partnership is where two individuals who are not close relatives but who have lived together for a minimum period of six months, register their relationship provided each is over 18 and neither is married nor in an existing civil partnership. One of the partners must be domiciled in England and Wales on the date of the application or have been resident during the year preceding it.

Chapter 9
Formalizing arrangements

Child arrangements for divorcing fathers

The court will not allow the divorce to proceed unless it is satisfied that adequate arrangements have been made for any 'relevant' children. The court will need to be satisfied as to the following:

- Where they are to live.
- With whom they are to live.
- What contact the other parent will have with them.
- Who will be looking after them on a day to day basis.
- What their health is like. If they need special arrangements because they are disabled, the court will want to know that these arrangements have been made.
- What their schooling arrangements are.
- Their maintenance.

It should be borne in mind that exact details may not be known at this time. For example, the home may have to be sold.

What is meant by the term 'relevant children'?

The court will be concerned with any child who was born to the parties, or who has been treated by the father as a child of the family, who is:

- Under 16 or
- Between 16 and 18 and still at college or at school full-time.

These are 'relevant children'. This includes adopted children and stepchildren but does not include foster children.

How does the Court know if the arrangements proposed are adequate?

When parties divorce, the party petitioning for a divorce, that is the Petitioner, will have to file at court the Divorce Petition together with a form known as a 'Statement of Arrangements for Children form'. In this form the Petitioner will set out the proposed arrangements for the children on divorce dealing with all the points upon which the court needs to be satisfied. The proposals will generally be that the children continue to live with the mother but have 'contact' with the father. The judge considers the arrangements for the children at the same time that he considers what is known as directions for trial, that is, at the same time he considers the divorce papers. If he approves the proposed arrangements a notice of satisfaction confirming this will be sent out to the parties.

How will the father find out what arrangements are being proposed?

If the wife is the Petitioner she will lodge her statement of arrangements for children form at court with her petition for divorce. She may agree the content of the form with the father before it is lodged, in which event an agreed form is lodged. A father will worry about committing himself to agreeing to the mother's proposals that he have 'contact', particularly where it is unclear what the exact contact arrangements are and what her definition of contact will be.

If an agreed form is not lodged, her statement of arrangements form will be served on the father with her divorce petition. He will receive what is known as an acknowledgment of service form with the petition. On that form there is a section asking whether he agrees with the petitioner's proposed arrangements for the children. If he does not he can file his own statement of arrangements form.

Agreeing the arrangements does not preclude a father from making an application to the court for an order reviewing those arrangements at a later date. For example, if subsequently problems develop or there is a change in circumstances making the current arrangements unworkable. The court will decide a particular issue at any given time. In other words, the statement of arrangements form is *not* a binding document.

If the father is the Petitioner this process will be the other way round.

If the judge does not approve the arrangements what will he do?

He may decide:

- He needs further information about the arrangements being proposed. For example, it may not be clear from the form who is looking after the children while the mother is at work.
- There should be an appointment for both parents to see him in Chambers. He may wish to clarify several points with them.
- A Family Court Reporter should prepare a report about the children. The Reporter will meet with both parents to talk about the proposals and talk to the children too. The report with the Reporter's recommendations will be sent to the court.
- The arrangements proposed should be in the form of a court order because this would be better for the children. An application for an order would then have to be made, but the court will only make an order if it would be better for the children than making no order at all.

Child arrangements for unmarried fathers

Their position is completely different. When unmarried parties split there are no formal requirements for the children and no statement of arrangements for children form is submitted to the court. The court is not involved and will not be unless an application is made to it to rule on the arrangements.

Deciding whether to make an application to the court

Considering the options

Having tried everything he can to reach an amicable arrangement with his estranged spouse or partner, a father has several options:

- Cave in and accept what he is being offered. In Part I we have looked at the reasons why fathers sometimes do this.
- Continue trying to come to an agreement with the mother without issuing court proceedings. As we saw in Chapter 2, he might try and enlist the support of third parties to help him. Many fathers state that this is only a short-term option. This is because mothers frequently move boundaries and promise to sort out the arrangements, thereby stringing matters out. The issues are not resolved between the parties because, so far as the father is concerned, the mother has no interest in resolving them. The parties may not even be communicating so there is no possibility of mediating and even if they are and they do, if they still cannot resolve the issues between them then the likelihood is that a court application will be made.
- Set out his requests formally, through a solicitor, and still try to reach an amicable agreement. By this stage fathers are generally resigned to having to issue proceedings. Unfortunately, the very fact that a father might instruct a solicitor to write a letter setting out his concerns and setting out his requests for contact is often enough to put the mother's back up and to inflame the situation. The father is in fact placed in an extremely difficult position; whatever he does he is caught.
- Issue court proceedings. An agreement can still be reached, but most fathers who find themselves in this position state that, as soon as they issue proceedings, mothers refuse to discuss matters as they feel the application is a personal attack upon them. All cases vary, however, and sometimes one party making an application may make the other party sit up and think about the implications of what they are doing and this gives them the impetus to resolve matters. Invariably matters proceed at least several stages before the matter is compromised anyway.

What are the objectives?

What does a father want to achieve and what are his long-term goals? If he is looking for flexibility, a court order will provide him with a rigid timetable to comply with, and any deviations from it may mean further applications to the court. If a mother is presented with a court timetable she may not be willing to consider any changes, telling the father that this is as a result of the court application that he made and he must accept it.

But if contact with his children is being severely limited then he may feel he has nothing to lose by making an application. Here a rigid timetable may be better because at least it would provide him with some contact. The most common question that fathers ask is, 'What is reasonable contact?' What can they expect from the court? We will look at this in Chapter 12.

Furthermore, any decision imposed by the court upon the father is going to be made by a judge who will adjudicate on the evidence put before him/her and how well the case is presented. How a father stands up to giving evidence will impact upon the outcome of the case. A criticism against judges – justified or not – is that they are biased against fathers and detached from reality. One father told me that he was advised not to proceed to court when it was discovered who the judge would be, on the basis that this judge was, as his barrister informed him, anti men and bad tempered as a result of suffering from arthritis. The whole point is that any control a father has over the decision-making process, in relation to probably one of the biggest decisions to affect his life, is passed to someone who does not know him or his children at all and only has a snapshot of his life. This is the reality no matter how much deliberation and consideration a judge may make over a decision and no matter how experienced that judge is. This is a hard call for fathers when they are relying upon the legal system to assist them.

An awkward case would be where the father has a degree of contact, or may even enjoy regular contact with his children, but seeks more and/or from time to time the mother goes into maternal gatekeeping mode. He may have reached an agreement with her but she chips away at it so that contact visits/times are topped and tailed or chopped about. He may find that she stops communicating with him over a number of the issues affecting the children and 'forgets' to give him information she would normally share with him. For example, she might decide to go away and leave the children with the nanny or the au pair and fail to inform him. In fact, any ongoing change in attitude should be looked at carefully because it can be the prelude to bigger problems. Fathers complain that mothers do not fully appreciate the meaning of joint parental responsibility and resent the fact that a non-resident father with parental responsibility will want to exercise that parental responsibility in relation to the children too. One father complained to me that his former wife held the view that, so far as she was concerned, since she had given birth to their daughter, she alone had parental responsibility. She refused to acknowledge that he did too and failed to consult him about important decisions relating to their daughter's welfare.

Before resorting to legal proceedings a father should find out about the legal process, the extent to which the legal process can help him achieve his goals but also its severe limitations. Many fathers who have been through the process and expended thousands of pounds, often exhausting their assets in the process, have little to show for it. They do not regard the process as 'father friendly' and see the courts as biased against them.

For fathers, the very idea of having to make an application to the court to see their own children and for a stranger to decide how often they can see them, is the most desperate scenario for them. Worst of all they feel totally helpless because, unable to reach an agreement with the mother, they have no choice but to apply to the court.

Chapter 10
Preparing your case for court

Automatic right to make an application or not?

We looked at the five main private law orders that are of particular interest to fathers in Chapter 6 and dealt specifically with parental responsibility in Chapter 8. As for residence, contact, prohibited steps or specific issue orders, the natural father has an automatic right to apply for any of these s8 orders, married or not. This does not include former parents who have had their child adopted. The unmarried father is entitled whether or not he has parental responsibility.

The following persons have an automatic right to apply for a residence or contact order, but if they want to apply for a prohibited steps or specific issue order, then they need the leave of the court, that is the permission of the court to make the application:

- A stepfather or stepmother who has treated the child as a child of the family.
- Any person with whom the child has lived for at least three years out of the last five years.
- Any person who has obtained the consent of all those people whose legal position would be affected, that is, anyone with parental responsibility or anyone with a residence order, or the local authority if the child is in care.

All other people not within the above require leave to apply for any order. For example, the natural parent of an adopted child would require leave.

Issuing proceedings

The Application itself

In practice, if a father has a solicitor acting for him, he/she will deal with the completion of all the necessary forms and send them to him for his approval. For a father acting in person, it is important he knows the procedure particularly as he will almost certainly have to deal with the mother's legal representatives.

If the father makes the application he is known as the Applicant and the other parties as Respondents. The application form will ask for details about the child or children in respect of whom he wants to apply for an order, his details, the other parties' details and brief details of the order for which he is applying. He must name as a Respondent every person whom he believes to have parental responsibility, and this is known as joining them as a party. The mother will be a Respondent. Other parties may apply to be joined, but the court will only join those who have a genuine interest in the child's welfare.

This form is submitted to the court together with sufficient copies for service and the court fee. On filing, the court fixes a date for a preliminary hearing or directions appointment. Copies of the application must be served on all Respondents at least 14 days before the hearing, together with a notice of proceedings form giving the date of the hearing and a blank acknowledgment of service form.

The Applicant must file a statement of service at court setting out how service was effected. This is because, if the other side fails to come to court, it is necessary to prove to the court that the other party has been given notice of the proceedings and the opportunity to present their case to the court and have not been prejudiced in any way.

Tell me about the proceedings.

The Respondent must complete the Acknowledgment form within 14 days of service, file it at court and serve a copy on the Applicant. The first court appointment is likely to be a conciliation appointment for the parties to try and agree the issues between them with the assistance of the court.

So far as conciliation court schemes are concerned, there is no uniform system and, although there are schemes in operation at divorce county courts and family proceedings courts, there are variations amongst the courts. The Principal Registry in London runs a conciliation scheme that deals with children's issues. When an application is issued, the first appointment takes place before a district judge sitting with a Family Court Reporter. The parties will be present as will their legal advisors. They will be encouraged to settle their dispute by negotiation. The appointment can be adjourned to enable the matter to be resolved.

If no agreement is reached, directions will be given as to how the case should proceed. Directions hearings enable courts to take firmer control of the timing of cases, admission of evidence and administration matters. The judge at the conciliation appointment will take no further part in the proceedings.

The Court may make a number of different directions. Some of the directions a court may make are as follows:
- That there be a timetable setting out the dates by which certain things need to be done and to which all parties must adhere. The courts are

conscious of delay being avoided in children's cases. We have already touched on the no-delay principle in Chapter 6.

- That a welfare report be prepared. The Children Act specifically provides that the court can provide a written or oral welfare report. This is the report that would have been prepared by the court welfare officer until CAFCASS became operational and the new title of Family Court Reporter was created. A report is not ordered in every case, but only where the court feels it needs one to assist it to make its decision. The Family Court Reporter will see the court file and interview both parents and the children. The FCR will want to see how both parents interact with the children and therefore to see each parent alone with the children in a home environment.

FCR's might also interview schoolteachers, the family doctor or grandparents, if their views are relevant. The report will then be prepared and generally this includes conclusions and recommendations about which order would be appropriate for the court to make. The report carries a lot of weight with the court. For the most part these statements are very conservative in their approach and there has been a lot of criticism that they are heavily weighted in favour of mothers.

- Submission of expert evidence. To protect children from unnecessary and repeated medical or psychiatric assessments, these are only allowed if the court gives permission. The court welfare report is generally the preferred step to take. If there is a particularly difficult medical problem with the child, that will have to be addressed by way of the appropriate expert report.

- Witness statements. Parties generally prefer for witness statements to be exchanged at the same time rather than one following on from the other. This avoids tit for tat allegations. Whatever the order made by the court, the court will control the time when this evidence is submitted. The statement is merely the written form of the oral evidence upon which a party intends to rely at court, and upon which the court makes its decision and therefore it must be accurate.

- The children's attendance. The court rules provide that the children must attend all proceedings, but in the children's interest the court can direct otherwise and use its discretion. For example, a very young child would not attend.

- Further hearing dates. Unless the case is resolved, at the end of every court hearing a date must be fixed for the next one. The parties cannot extend any time limit ordered by the court by mutual agreement. This is all part of the no-delay principle and gives the court control of the court timetable.

- The final hearing. We looked at this in Chapter 6. This will be held in chambers before the appropriate judge. The Applicant's barrister will open the case and call his witnesses to give evidence first: examination-in-chief. The Respondent's barrister will then ask those witnesses questions: cross-examination. The Respondent's barrister then calls his witnesses and the Applicant's barrister then cross-examines them. The Respondent's barrister then makes his closing speech followed by the Applicant's barrister.

- Judgment. This must be delivered as soon as possible after the hearing. Any order made must be in writing. Any findings of fact made by the court and the reasons for the decision will be kept on the court file. A copy of the order must be served on each party and on any person with whom the child is living.

What does it mean to make an application ex parte?

This means to make an application without notice to the other party. For example, it would be used in the case of an emergency where it is anticipated that the other parent intends to abduct the children as that parent has not returned them from a contact visit, or there is an urgent medical problem which needs to be addressed. We look at emergency applications in Chapter 13. If such an application is made, the full application should be filed either at the same time, or served on the Respondent within 48 hours after the making of the ex parte order.

The courts do not usually like to make ex parte residence/contact orders without hearing from the other party first. However, it may be possible to obtain an order from the court that the other party only receive short notice. In this way, there will be an earlier date for the hearing.

Can a child make an application for a s8 order?

A child will need the permission of the court if he/she wants to apply for a section 8 order and this will be given only if the court is satisfied that the child has sufficient understanding to make the application. The application will be for leave to apply and must be dealt with by the High Court.

A child will also need to obtain legal representation, funding for the case and to show that the merits of the case justify the order sought. If the court is of the view that the children's best interests would be served by having separate representation, a 'guardian ad litem' will be appointed. He/she will come from a special panel of individuals who have experience of dealing with and advising children and may have a social service background or be an ex-probation officer. A guardian ad litem will speak to the children and find out what they want and will usually appoint a solicitor to act for them but the children can also instruct their own solicitor.

What approach will the court take if an application for a s8 order is made?

In Chapter 6 we briefly considered the welfare principle, the 'no order' presumption and the 'no delay' principle:

The welfare principle

When a court determines any question with respect to the:
- upbringing of the child or
- administration of the child's property or the application of any income arising from it, the child's welfare shall be the court's paramount consideration.

The welfare factors

Before the Children Act came into force the only guidance on how to apply this principle was to be found in the case law. Now the court has a list of seven factors to which it refers when it is applying the welfare principle in contested s8 proceedings. The aim of the checklist is to provide a consistent approach for the Courts, the parties and advisors with which to work.

None of these factors is given any priority and the court is left to assess the relative importance of each factor in the circumstances of every case. If a father is applying for a residence order, he needs to show that the children are better off living with him: he will have to consider their physical needs, daily care and routine and see if what he can provide is better for his child, bearing in mind the court does not equate welfare with material wealth or the fact that one parent can offer more.

The checklist is not exhaustive and the court can also take any other relevant factors into account:

- **The ascertainable wishes and feelings of the child concerned (considered in the light of the child's age and understanding).**
  We have already referred to the welfare report and this is one of the ways in which the child's wishes and feelings can be made known to the court. The report should consider the child's wishes, as well as the maturity of the child, and the extent to which the parents may have exerted influence over the child in forming any views. A court is not obliged to follow the suggestions made in the report.

  A judge may interview a child privately during the case to form his own opinion, but this is uncommon and will not be done in relation to a child under eight years old. The child's wishes do not always take precedence and the court may feel that the child's wishes are not in his/her best interests.

Another issue to consider involving a child's welfare is the extent to which a child can consent to or refuse medical treatment. If a child is sufficiently mature he can consent to treatment and only the court can override his consent.

- **The child's physical, emotional and educational needs.**
This focuses on the child and looks at accommodation, medical needs and education, as well as how close the child is to brothers and sisters and others with whom he may lose touch if a particular order is made. The court considers circumstances very carefully before splitting brothers and sisters. It would be unusual to separate siblings close in age but where there is a large age gap it has happened particularly where the children are already living with a different parent.

- **The likely effect on the child of any change in circumstances.**
If the current arrangements for a child are working satisfactorily, the court will be unlikely to change them. This attitude is often referred to as maintaining the status quo and means the person with whom the child is living, generally the mother, is at a considerable advantage. This is one of the major problems for fathers to overcome because it is very difficult to shift the court from this starting point. Continuity of care is considered as the most important part of a child's sense of security, and disruption of a child's routine is to be avoided if at all possible. The court will look at all changes in the child's circumstances. For example, if another adult is going to be introduced into the child's life because one parent is to remarry or cohabit with someone new or the child is going to have to move to a new home or school.

Fathers also worry because they know that in most cases the longer the status quo is maintained the harder it is to change it and if there are delays they will be more prejudiced. The philosophy behind the Children Act is that any delay is likely to prejudice the child and therefore a timetable is imposed. Ironically, once proceedings have started this may help, but fathers complain that very often the reason why they issued proceedings was because the mother dragged her feet in sorting out the contact and continually moved the boundary lines.

- **The child's age, sex, background and any characteristics of the child which the court considers relevant.**
A child's age is significant, and courts invariably order that very young babies live with their mothers. A teenager can generally cope with living with either parent. Age also has a decisive influence on the importance a court will attach to a child's wishes. There is no presumption of law that a child of any age should be with one parent or the other. The sex

of a child may be taken into account. If children are from a multi-racial background, then the court will need to look at this background and how they have been brought up and what influence both parents' culture has had on the children to date. The same applies where the parents come from a different religious background.

- **Any harm that the child has suffered or was at risk of suffering.**
This will cover any past or future harm to the child. Harm is a very broad term and will cover both physical and psychological injury. The court also considers the harm caused to a child by not seeing both parents. Contact is the right of the child, not of the parent. The child has a right to know his other parent. This is something mothers find very hard to deal with in these circumstances.

- **How capable each of the child's parents and any other person in relation to whom the court considers the question relevant is of meeting the child's needs.**
This factor involves the court looking at the parents or other proposed carers to assess their ability to care for the child. The parent's conduct will be relevant to the extent that it may affect their suitability as a parent. If a father has a criminal record that will be a factor the court will consider.

In disputes between natural parents and another, for example a grandparent, the courts tend to presume that unless there is positive evidence to the contrary it is in the children's best interests to live with their natural parents.

Whether a parent works will influence the care of the child. The parent's lifestyle and sexual orientation may be relevant. A parent who suffers from mental or physical illness, which could mean sudden or long-term stays in hospital, might also be less suitable as a full-time carer.

If a parent is proposing to share care with someone else, that person's capabilities will also be considered. This means that new partners or spouses, relatives and friends may be relevant as well as nannies and child minders.

- **The range of powers available to the court under this act and proceedings in question.**
This factor encourages the court to think laterally and to consider every option open to it including that of making no order at all. The court has the power to make any order in favour of any person irrespective of who has applied. For example, in the course of a residence application the court may decide it is better for the child to live with a grandparent even though the grandparent may not have been a party to the application.

The no-order presumption

As we have seen, the court will not make an order unless it considers that doing so would be better for the child than making no order at all. The reasoning behind this is one of non-intervention and the belief that, in the main, parents know what is right for their children and will act in their best interests.

Where an order would definitely be made
Where there is a real danger that one parent may abduct the child, it would be an advantage to have in operation the restrictions on removal from the UK contained in a residence order.

Avoidance of delay

The court must have regard to the general principle that any delay in determining the question is likely to prejudice the welfare of the child. To a child one year is a long time. A child's sense of time is very different from that of an adult. The court is required to draw up a timetable and give directions to enable it to deal with the matter without delay.

How long will the order last for?

A section 8 order will cease to have effect when the child reaches 16, but the court does have power in exceptional circumstances to make or extend an order beyond a child's 16th Birthday. In any event, it will cease when the child reaches 18. If a residence or contact order is made in favour of a parent these orders will automatically end if the child's parents live together for a continuous period of more than 6 months.

Public law

Implications for fathers with children taken into care

Public law is a vast area and relates to the involvement of the local authority and care proceedings. The various orders that can be made are not within the scope of this book save for their effect upon a father's contact with a child of his in care.

The local authority has taken the child into care but the father wants contact. Is he entitled?

Contact with the family is in the best interests of a child in care unless proved otherwise. Contact with children in care is subject to the control of the court.

When a care order is made in relation to children, those children should maintain contact with their parents if at all possible. A child in care is afforded reasonable contact with parents, guardians, or anyone with a residence order in force immediately before the care order was made.

If contact is not forthcoming a father could make an application for contact. However, an application can only be made once in every six months, unless the leave of the court is obtained. But if a father is using the application in effect as a means by which he can obtain the return of the child it is unlikely to succeed, especially if the matter has already been fully dealt with by the court.

Although the local authority has a duty to promote contact between the parents and any other person having parental responsibility, it does not have to do so if this is not reasonably practicable or in line with what is in the best interests of the child. The court has to weigh up the pros and cons as to whether continued contact is in the child's best interests. Where a child is in care and an application for contact is made, the court carries out a balancing exercise and weighs up all the factors.

It has been said that contact must not be allowed to destabilize or endanger or frustrate the arrangements planned for the child. The court can require the local authority to justify long-term plans if those plans exclude contact with a parent! The local authority or the child can apply to the court for an order that a 'named' person should have such contact with the child as the court considers appropriate. This includes power to authorize the authority to refuse contact to a named party.

In exercising its discretion to determine issues related to future contact, the court should have regard to the child's welfare as paramount and to the long-term plans of the authority for the child's future. At the end of the day contact should continue, but it is evident that so far as children in care are concerned there are a number of hurdles to overcome.

Chapter 11
Residence

The question of residence

The primary carer

Mothers are still expected to be the primarily responsible parent and to have residence of the children following a divorce or relationship breakdown.

Fathers face a Catch 22 situation when it comes to their residence claims. The fact is that most fathers work full time and often very long hours, and this is used against them to defeat their claims. It is argued that, from a purely practical point of view, the children should remain with their mother. However, as we looked at in Chapter 1, the family unit is changing and so are arrangements for the care of children.

Although fathers generally have to work to continue to support the family whether the parties are together or apart, there are many mothers who work full-time and the children are cared for by nannies/child minders. What difference would it make if it were the other way round? Could it be argued that if a father does not have to work or could make arrangements for the children to be cared for while he is working that he could succeed in an application for a residence order? As we have seen, a father who is self-employed would be in a very good position to care for the children. What about the scenario where the father is a 'house husband?'

A recent case – heavily reported in the media – related to a 'house husband' who for a considerable period of time had been the primary carer of the children and wanted residence of them. In this case the mother was the breadwinner and had a very lucrative career in the city. The mother decided she wanted to give up her career and take over the full-time care of the two children aged six and three until the younger of the two went to school. In addition to that she wanted to take the children out of their fee-paying London day schools and to move to Linlithgow sending the children to state schools there. By the time the matter came to court the child-care arrangements had changed to shared parenting. The judge at first instance ruled in favour of the mother and consequently the father sought leave to appeal to the Court of Appeal.

It was argued on behalf of the father that the judge had acted on gender discrimination. If the roles had been reversed and it was the father who wanted to give up his position in the City, with the direct consequence that this would create financial hardship for the family, it would certainly not have persuaded the judge to make an order in his favour. The Court of Appeal decided that, on balance, the mother's reasons for giving up work were genuine; she had based her proposals for residence and contact on an in depth consideration of what would be the best solution for the children and her proposals were actually better for the children than those of the father. The problem for the father was that he had based his proposals on the mother continuing to earn a lucrative wage in the City and when it was clear that that would no longer be the case, his proposals fell away. Lord Justice Thorpe, one of the Court of Appeal Judges, rejected the submissions made by the father's Counsel. Leave to Appeal was refused by the Court of Appeal.

Fathers' rights organizations were angered at the decision which they regard as a regressive step for fathers. This has sparked a number of articles in the press about a father's role, and whether a father can be as good as a mother if their roles are reversed. Lawyers state that the decision does not mean all future cases will follow this decision, and emphasize that each and every case is decided on its own facts and merits, and that when the judge comes to exercise his/her discretion the welfare of the children must come first. However, fathers are questioning exactly what those facts and merits have to be to acquire residence, and that this does not bode well for shared residence either. We look at the impact and implications of this decision in Chapter 15.

The non-resident father

Fathers say that it is not just the fact that the children live with their mother that causes problems but the attitude that goes with the status of being 'the non-resident parent'. They assert that mothers believe they are more important than fathers, and that fathers are made to feel as if they are second class citizens, lucky even to be allowed to have contact with their children. This is why something needs to be done about the whole concept of being the 'non-resident' parent. Because a father does not generally have residence, contact with his children becomes very precious and if the contact is restricted, then it is obvious that he will push for it and will be aggrieved if he is thwarted at every turn.

Applying for residence

There are many cases where the father could press for residence of the children but does not do so as it would mean dragging up undesirable details relating to the mother's past, and because he is advised that an application presented in such terms would not bode well with the court. One father told me he was advised in no uncertain terms by Counsel that dredging up these details would not put him in a favourable light with the court, and since he was unlikely to succeed in his application anyway then he was best to forget it.

In this case the mother was an alcoholic and regularly went off on drinking binges. She was not really capable of looking after the child, a boy aged twelve, whom the father had looked after since he was a baby. The father genuinely wanted his son to live with him because he feared for his safety and considered making a residence application. The father had his own business and was able to devote time to his son's upbringing. The divorce was particularly acrimonious. The father felt it would be in his son's best interests if he had residence, but he did not want his son to be caught in the crossfire and because he was strongly advised 'to forget any thoughts of applying for residence' he did not make the application. Furthermore, he knew his ex-wife would bitterly contest any application and their relationship would deteriorate further. He was in a very difficult position.

At the financial hearing an extremely unfavourable settlement was ordered on the basis that the son was to live with the mother. The assets in the case were tight and the father was effectively left high and dry. Since then, the son has moved in with his father anyway and the father has been left trying to unravel the financial settlement. Nearly five years down the line he feels particularly dissatisfied with the way the legal process treated him. There are many fathers like him.

In the majority of cases the question of residence is therefore decided between the parties and no application for an order is made. Nearly all these cases result in the mother obtaining residence.

What are the implications of a residence order?

The court is given wide powers to attach directions, conditions, incidental and supplementary provisions to a residence order. These might include directing that the non-resident parent be informed about where the child is to be educated, and any medical treatment the child requires where, for example, the parent with whom the child is living has religious objections to blood transfusions.

When a residence order has been made there are two aspects of parental responsibility which are automatically affected. They are name changes and removing a child from the jurisdiction.

Name changes

When children are born it is convention that leads to them being known by the father's surname when the parents are married or living together, and by the mother's name when she is unmarried and living apart from the father. A child's surname may be changed by:
- The parents or those with parental responsibility.
- By the mature child him/herself.
- With leave of the court.
- By adoption of the child.

Where a residence order is in force a child cannot be called by a new surname without either the written consent of every person who has parental responsibility or the leave of the court. Where there is joint parental responsibility the same conditions apply regardless of whether there is a residence order. The implication is that changing a child's forename is not restricted in the same way as his/her surname.

If the mother wants to change the child's surname she has to obtain the father's permission and if he refuses it she will have to apply to the court. The court's decision will be based on the welfare principle, and once again the welfare of the child will be the paramount consideration. It has to be in the child's best interests. This is an area where the case law is changing all the time. However, there are some general principles to be followed:
- If the parents are married they both have a power and duty to register their child's name.
- If they are unmarried the mother has the sole duty and power to do so.
- After registration of a child's name, the grant of a residence order obliges any person wishing to change the surname to obtain the leave of the court or the written consent of all those who have parental responsibility.
- In the absence of a residence order, the person wishing to change the surname from that registered has to obtain the relevant written consent of all those who have parental responsibility or the leave of the court by making an application for a specific issue order.
- On any application the welfare of the child is paramount.
- Among the factors to which the court should have regard is the registered surname of the child and the reasons for the registration; for instance, recognition of the biological link with the child's father. Registration is always a relevant and important consideration but it is not in itself decisive.
- Relevant considerations should include factors which could arise in the future as well as the present.
- Reasons given for changing or seeking to change a child's name based on the fact that the child's name is not the same as the parent making

the application does not generally carry that much weight.

- The reasons for an earlier unilateral decision to change a child's name might be relevant.
- Any change of circumstances of the child since the original registration might be relevant.
- In the case of a child whose parents were married to each other the fact of the marriage is important and there would have to be strong reasons to change the name from the father's surname if the child was so registered.
- Where the child's parents were not married to each other the mother has control over registration. Consequently, on an application to change the surname of the child the degree of commitment of the father to the child, the quality of contact if it occurred between father and child, the existence or absence of parental responsibility are all relevant factors to be taken into account.

Removing a child from the jurisdiction

Where a residence order has been made no person may remove the child from the UK without either the written consent of every person who has parental responsibility or leave of the court.

Holidays or short periods

The Children Act allows the person in whose favour a residence order has been made to take the child out of the UK for periods of less than one month without consent. So if the children live with their mother and she has a residence order she can take them abroad as many times as she likes provided each individual trip does not last more than one month.

The father, on the other hand, as the parent without the residence order, needs to seek consent every time he wants to take the children abroad for whatever period. To avoid him having to make repeated applications to the court, at the time the residence order is granted the court can add a direction allowing him to take the children out of the country. If he lives abroad this means that regular trips for his children to stay with him will be permitted, without having to go to the mother every time to request her consent to the trip.

If this proviso is not included and an application to obtain consent has to be made, the court will base its decision on the welfare principle. If a father wants to take his child on holiday abroad then it would not be difficult to persuade the court that this would be in the child's best interests, unless the mother can show that the holiday is being used as a cover for abduction.

If there is no residence order in force then in theory either party can take their children abroad without any restriction or need for consent. However, the parent proposing the trip could be prevented from taking the children by the other parent obtaining a prohibited steps forbidding the children being taken abroad if there is a real threat that the other parent does not intend to return them. Additionally, a criminal offence will be committed by the parent or any other person removing the children if the permission of the other parent or the court is not obtained. The offences will be committed under the Child Abduction Act 1984.

Leaving the country permanently

This is one of the possibilities that fathers dread. Many of the cases involve mothers who have remarried and wish to relocate with their new husband or where the new husband is a foreign national. There are also cases where the mother is a foreign national and after the parties split she wishes to return 'home' to her family.

For the mother to do this she will need to apply for leave to remove the children. Although many mothers succeed in their applications to remove, more fail, and this has increasingly become the trend in recent years. However, there has been a controversial case recently which has caused alarm for fathers and this relates to a father whose ex-wife wished to relocate to Australia with her 'alleged' lesbian lover and was granted leave to do so. This has sparked debate because it raises the issue about children being brought up by two female parents and whether that is in their best interests, but also because on making its decision the court has to consider a number of factors. These include whether the mother has any family connection with the country to which she wishes to relocate and what she is going to do for financial support after she has done so. In this case it was acknowledged that the mother would be reliant on her Australian 'partner' for financial support but the parties denied that that they were lesbians and the court accepted their word. The question as to whether it would be in the children's best interests to be brought up by them was not considered by the court.

The court considers the following factors on such an application:

- It will review the welfare checklist. The court does not have to go through every factor but it must direct itself to the list. It will want to know the children's thoughts and feelings on the matter. What have they been told? Do they understand the implications of moving so far away in terms of the contact with their father? Have they been able to talk to him about it? Will they suffer harm as a result of losing contact and if so, is that sufficient reason to refuse the application?
- The leave of the court should not be withheld unless the interests of the

child and those of the parent with care are clearly incompatible. Previously the courts held that the mother should be allowed to relocate because she might become unhappy if not allowed to do so and that this might adversely affect the child. But this should only be taken into account if the overall proposal is reasonable.

- Contact. Are the current contact arrangements good or not and will the mother help maintain the contact? How is this going to be maintained? When direct contact cannot take place, what about indirect contact and how much will all this cost? This is a supremely important consideration. Fathers argue that on paper mothers' proposals may seem feasible and workable but that in reality, once the children are abroad, particularly if they are thousands of miles away, those proposals will go out the window.
- Checklist of matters. Has the mother really thought this all through and made proper arrangements for the children? She must give convincing reasons for uprooting the children and her proposals must be realistic. Has she considered:
- Schooling. Availability? Suitability?
- School holidays. These may be completely different in the country she is moving to and contact could be limited on that basis alone.
- Child care arrangements if the mother is going to work full time.
- Housing. Availability? Suitability? Location?
- Her contact proposals. Realistic?
- Employment. Is she working and if so, what will she be doing?
- Language problems.
- Her new partner. What is his relationship like with the children? Degree of commitment? How solid is the new relationship? What is his attitude? This may have an effect on the contact.

For a father faced with the possibility of the mother of his children emigrating and wanting to take the children with her, this will be a nerve-racking time.

There is another scenario where the mother does not emigrate but decides to move to the other end of the UK. At least in a situation where the mother is emigrating, the father has the opportunity to put his case when the mother makes her application for leave to remove the child from the UK. If she moves within the UK he does not have this opportunity. For example, a father might be further away or just as far away from his children in the UK than a father whose children are in Northern Europe, but can do very little about it. What is more, if he does not have the money to pay for the cost of travel to see them, the contact will be severely limited.

In one case the parties were not married but had a daughter. They separated when the daughter was about two years old and mother and daughter went to live with the maternal grandparents. Due to her work commitments the mother had to move away but left her daughter with the grandmother. The father accepted this. The mother and the father saw their daughter on alternate weekends. They had a very amicable relationship and were always able to agree any issues relating to her, and thereby act in her best interests.

The mother then began a relationship with another man. She married him and she had another daughter. Her new husband lived in the Middle East so she moved there with her new daughter. She wanted the daughter from her previous relationship to move there too, so that she and her new half-sister could be together. Her elder daughter, now aged six, missed her mother very much and became withdrawn, unhappy and her schoolwork suffered. She said she wanted to live with her mother but at the same time wanted to keep close contact with her father and grandmother. She thought that if she moved to be with her mother that she would still see them at weekends.

The father was absolutely devoted to his daughter and made it clear that although it would make him very sad if his daughter went to the Middle East, if this was something that she really wanted and would make her happy, he was prepared to let her go. This is an unusual case because fortunately the parties have an excellent relationship and have remained friends. The mother actively encourages contact and has always done so. The reality is of course that the distance between father and daughter will limit the physical contact but the mother promotes telephone contact and the daughter returns to the UK for the summer holidays. This case is an example of how a mother's attitude has a direct bearing upon the future contact and relationship that a father is able to maintain with his child in a situation where the mother relocates.

Chapter 12
Contact

Reasonable contact

What is reasonable contact?

What one father may regard as reasonable contact may not be so to another father, but generally, whatever the level of contact it is not enough. Unfortunately the law may not grant the father the contact he considers to be reasonable. A father would be regarded as having very reasonable contact if he had contact every other weekend, telephone contact during the week and a couple of weeks holiday contact in the Summer and the rest of the holiday time split, although not necessarily equally.

When the parent's relationship breaks down it is important to minimize disruption to the children but if they have a loving relationship with their father then the benefits of that to them, and the continuity of contact with him, will far outweigh any negative aspects. The reality is that after separation children's routines are going to be disrupted anyway, as instead of having one base they will have two, a direct consequence of their parents splitting up. But the disruption can be limited by the parents and, at the end of the day, what is important is to build healthy relationships. If a father does not have a sufficient degree of contact once he and the mother part, it is harder to build up the relationship with his children and they lose out.

Those advising fathers against the backdrop of contested divorce and/or financial proceedings, often recommend the father to 'back–off' and not press the mother on contact issues until the whole situation simmers down. Fathers are therefore placed in the unenviable position of having to wait to resolve matters, which in turn can cause frustration and encourage conflict and resentment because, once again, this leaves him in a no-win situation and subject to the whims of the mother.

Starting point

The starting point is that the child has a right to know both parents and should have contact with his/her father. It is not the other way round. However, there is a presumption of contact between parents and their children. The same presumption does not apply between children and their stepparents.

The court will consider the circumstances and the welfare of the child will always be the paramount consideration. The court is only concerned with the parents' interests insofar as they affect the welfare of the child and will refer to the welfare checklist of seven factors we looked at in detail in Chapter 10.

The form of contact

The court has a wide and comprehensive jurisdiction to make contact orders. It can order for direct contact or indirect contact to take place and can attach conditions to the contact.

Direct contact

This means seeing and being with the children and includes telephone contact. The amount of contact can either be specified in the order or the order could be for 'reasonable' contact in which case the arrangements can be made between the parents. However, this can be unsatisfactory because the definition of 'reasonable' is in itself unclear and can be abused by a mother wishing to be awkward.

Where there is an order for direct contact there has to be a positive obligation on the parent who is to allow contact to take place. This is important from the point of view of enforcing the order. The order should state that the mother 'must make the children available for contact' with the father rather than to say that he is 'to have contact with the children'. The difference between the two is that the former is enforceable, in principle at least if not in practice, and we look at this below.

There is no set format for the order. It depends upon the case. It may set out times and dates and there may be conditions attached to the contact or to enable contact to take place.

If a father has not seen his child for some time, for example, in a situation where there has been violence, the order may contain conditions and directions for the contact to be built up gradually. The contact could be supervised and would probably take place at a local contact centre. Where this is ordered there has to be a contact referral by the solicitors to both parties which has to be delivered to the contact centre by the Applicant's solicitor. The National Association of Child Contact Centres (NACC) has a protocol for referrals.

Indirect contact

This could be by letter, cards or photographs, for example. There might be a direction that the absent father should be sent school progress reports and any cards or letters he sends to the child be read to the child. An order of this nature would stipulate that the mother was to allow the father to have indirect contact with the father.

In one case the father was American and his wife was English but was working in America where they met. They married, and moved to the UK and had a daughter. The relationship broke down when their daughter was eighteen months old. The mother remained in the UK and went to live with her parents; the father's employment contract came to an end and he returned to the USA to work. The end of the relationship was very acrimonious and the mother and her family were hostile to contact and determined to limit contact as much as possible.

The father only had two weeks holiday a year and tried to organize his flights to the UK so that he would come over on a Friday and return home on a Monday, thereby carving out ten contact visits a year. He would book his flights well in advance and agree the dates with the mother but the mother would change the arrangements at the last minute. When he did see his daughter he had to go to her parents' house, was never left alone with her, the argument being that he was 'a stranger' to her as she had been so tiny when the parties had separated. The opportunity to develop a meaningful father/daughter relationship was denied. The problem was ongoing.

When the matter came to a head and the father made an application to the court the daughter was aged three. The father explained his predicament and how his attempts to see his daughter were constantly being thwarted by the mother. The District Judge said that the child was very young and that the father should send her a card on her Birthday and that he could telephone his daughter even though it was evident to everyone that it was unlikely he would ever manage to speak with his daughter. The father was devastated. He indicated that, at the hearing, the District Judge was not interested in listening to his arguments about how hostile the mother was to contact, but took pains to accommodate her at every level and accepted her 'reasons' for limiting the contact. Unsurprisingly, he went away with no confidence in the system whatsoever.

What happens where there has been domestic violence?

This topic is worthy of a whole book in its own right as it is such an important issue. However, it is not within the bounds of this book to deal with the issues relating to domestic violence in depth but, because of its direct relevance to the question of contact, and since it is one of the most common reasons why a mother refuses to comply with a contact order, it must be addressed.

Where there has been a history of domestic violence between the parents this will impact on the court's decision on the level of contact granted. This is the case even though the child has not been physically harmed. For example, it may be that after the parties split the mother argues she is concerned that on contact visits the father might be violent towards the children. Furthermore, she may also be afraid that he may be violent towards her again if she is not compliant over contact.

On 12 April 2000 the Lord Chancellor's Department issued a Report on the issue of contact between children and violent parents. It set out proposed good practice guidelines for courts dealing with cases in which domestic violence is raised as a reason for the refusal of contact or for that contact to be limited. The Government accepted the Guidelines. The Report was based upon the responses to a Consultation Paper issued the previous year. The definition of 'domestic violence' used by the Paper covered physical, sexual or emotional abuse.

Although there is no presumption against contact, where domestic violence is proven to have taken place, the court has historically exercised its discretion as to the level of contact awarded. The court has always considered negative factors. These are the seriousness of the violence, the risks involved, the impact on the child (that is the effect that exposure to domestic violence between the parents has had on the child), the impact on the residential parent and the motivation of the parent seeking contact. These negative factors have been balanced against positive factors and consideration given to the recognition by the violent parent of past conduct and that parent's commitment to change.

Under the Guidelines, where there has been a finding of domestic violence the Court is recommended to consider all the above. Careful consideration has to be given to the motivation of the parent pursuing contact. Does the parent genuinely believe it is in the best interests of the child for contact to take place, or is it just a way to continue the campaign of harassment, intimidation or violence against the other parent?

Having made an order that there should be contact even though domestic violence has taken place, the court then has to decide on the form of contact. For example, the court may decide that direct contact is in the best interests of the child but that it should be supervised. Conditions may be attached to the order. If a father is violent because he is an alcoholic, one of the conditions may be that he seeks treatment for his alcoholism. Contact may be for a set period and a date given for the order to be reassessed.

The Guidelines state that on an application for interim contact where the allegations of domestic violence have not been decided upon as yet, the court should give particular consideration to the likely risk of harm to the child. 'Harm' covers physical or emotional harm. This applies whether contact is granted or refused. The court should ensure, so far as it can, that any risk of harm to the child is minimized and that the safety of the child and the residential parent is secured before, during and after any such contact.

The Adoption & Children Act amends the Children Act to include the recognition of the harm that children can suffer by actually witnessing domestic violence. This means that in all cases where the court considers the welfare checklist the courts will have to decide if domestic violence has taken place and, if so, what the likely harm is to the child at the present time and in the future. This should mean more protection for the children.

Where there has been child abuse, individual circumstances should be taken into consideration, and if there is documented proof of abuse or irresponsible behaviour, the courts should be free to make their decisions accordingly. It is a sad fact that each year thousands of fathers are falsely accused of child abuse. Mothers use this as a means by which contact can be prevented. However, proof of the child abuse must be shown. Time wasted on cases where false allegations are made means less time devoted to genuine cases where children really need protection.

No contact at all

A contact order can also be made preventing contact with someone. Another way of achieving this is to obtain a prohibited steps order, and we look at this in more detail in the next Chapter.

In deciding whether contact should cease or be reintroduced, the court will apply the principle that no court should deprive any child of contact to either parent unless it is wholly satisfied that it is in the interest of the child that contact should cease. This is a conclusion at which the court is extremely slow to arrive. It would be a very drastic order because, as we have seen, it is usually deemed in the best interests of a child to have contact with the father.

Enforcing contact

There are two aspects to this, and these are making an application to court for a contact order where the father's contact is limited and making an application to enforce the contact order.

By making an application for a contact order

For some, once the order is made, that is sufficient and the parties do manage to comply with it even though their own relationship is still very strained. However, it may be necessary to make further applications if other issues arise or there are changes in circumstances and the parties cannot agree these between themselves.

By making an application to enforce the contact order

A father faces a predicament where he has obtained a contact order but the mother still refuses to allow contact to proceed. He probably applied for an order for contact in the first place because the mother was seriously sabotaging contact. Unfortunately for some fathers, the sabotage does not cease merely by the fact that a court order is in existence. These are situations where the mother is totally opposed to contact. The mother is termed implacable or hostile to contact. There are various ways to enforce an order under the current law.

What can be done?

If the court is satisfied that the mother has not given the child up for contact, it could make an order authorizing an Officer of the court or a constable to take charge of the child and deliver the child to the father. The whole scenario is very unsatisfactory from a practical point of view and could cause more harm than good for the child. This is why mothers who are determined to block contact are able to do so effectively, because judges are very reluctant to make an order which could be detrimental to a child. This clearly makes the current law redundant to some extent and this is no more apparent when it comes to committing a mother to prison (referred to below).

Penalties for breaching the contact order

In the County Court and High Court the breaking of a Court Order is known as a 'contempt of court'. The penalty for this can be:

- Imprisonment or committal.
- A fine.
- For the contemnor's (that is the one in contempt) assets to be sequestrated – this means that they are frozen.

Although freezing the assets can be useful where the contemnor has gone abroad, in child abduction cases the court is more likely to order committal. Before any committal order can be made the court has to be satisfied beyond reasonable doubt that the defendant knowingly broke the order. Furthermore, the requirement is that a penal notice must have been attached to the Order in question. A penal notice is a notice informing the person against whom the order is made that a failure to obey it constitutes a contempt of court for which the offender may be sent to prison.

The courts regard these as remedies of last resort. These are provocative and emotional applications and could be very damaging. It is important not to lose sight of the child's welfare. If the mother is totally hostile to contact the court must look carefully at her reasons. Even if a mother is found to be unreasonably hostile, the courts are very unwilling to lock up mothers who refuse to comply with contact because of the impact this will have upon the child. The court can impose costs penalties instead – but this is not particularly satisfactory either. Where is the money for this going to come from? The court would not want to deprive a mother of money she needs for her child. But for a father trying to enforce contact this is totally unsatisfactory. What recourse is there for him?

The whole area of enforcement of contact orders is highly contentious and it is one of the areas about which numerous recommendations were made to the Lord Chancellor in the Report *Making Contact Work*. We look at what these recommendations are in Chapter 15.

Chapter 13
Emergency procedures

Prohibited steps order

We looked at the definition of a prohibited steps order in Chapter 6. The first point to note is that the court cannot make a prohibited steps order if the purpose behind it is to achieve a result that could be achieved by a residence or contact order. It is easier to demonstrate by example exactly what can be achieved by this order.

Where a prohibited steps order would be appropriate

- In an abduction case, if the father has abducted the child and the result required is for the abducted child to be returned to the mother, the correct order for her to seek is a residence order with appropriate conditions and directions preventing unauthorized removal.
- If the child is living with the mother and she abducts the child and the required result is to obtain the return of the child to the UK and to prevent further removal of the child, then a prohibited steps order is the correct order to obtain. The child will nevertheless remain living with the mother.
- If no residence order were in force, a prohibited steps order could be used to prohibit the removal of the child from the country or prevent a change of surname. We looked at changes of name and removal from the jurisdiction in Chapter 11.
- If a father wants to obtain an order preventing a child from living with someone else, the correct order would be a residence order.
- Sometimes it is difficult to know which would be the most appropriate order and it really does depend on circumstances. In one case where the mother's cohabitee had abused the children, the court decided that a 'negative' contact order preventing the mother from allowing contact would only afford partial protection. The court made a prohibited steps order against the cohabitee instead.
- If an order is needed to restrict publicity, a prohibited steps order is not the appropriate order. This is because a prohibited steps order can only relate to matters which are included within parental responsibility and publicity is not one of these matters. This would be covered by the wider powers of wardship and dealt with by the High Court.

Specific issue order

We looked briefly at specific issue orders in Chapter 6. A father would need to apply for a specific issue order where he disagrees with a decision the mother has made in relation to a specific issue and which they cannot resolve between themselves. In the same way as a prohibited steps order, a specific issue order cannot be used to achieve 'back door' residence or contact orders.

Where a specific issue order would be appropriate

The following are examples of specific issue orders:
- For the court to decide which school the child should attend because the parents cannot agree.
- For the court to decide whether the child should have a particular operation or course of treatment.
- The religion the child should adopt.
- If it is desired to prevent anyone having contact with the child, this seems to be the appropriate order to obtain as it is accepted that a contact order can only authorize contact and not prevent it. However, it has been held that the court could make a contact order providing for no contact. The person with whom the child lives could be prevented therefore from allowing contact with an abusing parent or someone else the court considered was harming the child in any way.

Child abduction

Basics

Child abduction is a huge topic which also merits its own book. This is an area where a father should seek advice from a solicitor on the Child Abduction Panel, as the law is complicated.

In Chapter 11 we looked at residence orders and the effect of a residence order where a party wants to take a child abroad as well as applications for leave to remove a child from the jurisdiction, but the important issue is when the removal of a child becomes an abduction matter.

Authorized removal or abduction?

- If a residence order is in force, it may have conditions attached to it about removing the child. The court can enforce the conditions by an order that the child be produced to the parent with the residence order.
- If there is no residence order in force, an ex parte application for a

residence order or prohibited steps order could be applied for and then enforced by the court. The court has power to order anyone who may have information as to a child's whereabouts to disclose it to the court.

- If the child is removed from England to another part of the UK, this enables a s8 order to be recognized and enforced by a local court. The order has to be registered.
- If a mother has a residence order, the father will commit an offence if he does not have her consent or the permission of the court to remove the child. She will not commit an offence if she removes the child unless they are away for more than one month and it is clear they are not on their way back.
- Where there is no residence order in force and the father removes the child no offence is committed 'initially' but this will become a criminal offence if he refuses to return the child. In any event, it is a criminal offence for any person except a person with parental responsibility to take a child from any person without lawful authority or reasonable excuse.

Preventative measures

Port alert procedures

If there is an imminent threat of abduction (that is within the next 24 to 48 hours) then the port alert procedure can be used. The authorities will need a full description of the child who is travelling, the likely abductor, likely destination, and photographs. Curiously enough, there is no need for a s8 order to have been obtained if the child is under 16 although if there is an order in existence it should be produced to the police. On the other hand, the system is only available for children over 16 if a s8 order exists.

Passports

If a father wants an order preventing the issue/surrender of a passport, he can only obtain it if there is already in existence an order prohibiting or restricting the removal of the child from the UK. As part of an order there may be a direction that the child's passport be lodged with the other party's solicitor if there is a threat of abduction.

Remedies

Although a criminal offence will be committed if a child is abducted abroad, it will not bring about the return of the child. The Hague Convention of Civil Aspects of Child Abduction 1980 and the European Convention of Recognition and Enforcement of Decisions Concerning

Custody of Children 1980 provide procedures for tracing a child and for their return. If the other party has taken the child to another country it may be possible to obtain the child's return, but this depends upon the country.

Convention countries

If the child has been removed unlawfully to a convention country without the other parent's consent and wrongfully retained there, the Convention will be able to help with the return of the child. The Hague Convention provides that the Central Authority of the country to which the child has been taken must help the parent find the child and protect the child once found. If a child is abducted, a parent must take immediate action as after one year the return of the child becomes more difficult, although it does not mean that a return is impossible.

Non-convention countries

Where a child is abducted to a non-convention country such as Saudi Arabia, for example, then the court is free to determine the case on its merits under the wardship jurisdiction, although it will commonly have regard to the factors specified in the Hague Convention in reaching its decision. The court may make the child/children wards of court and order the abductor to return the children to the jurisdiction. If the abductor fails to do so, the court may make an order that the abductor is in contempt of court and can then make an order freezing the abductor's assets in the UK, that is sequestrate them. If the abductor returned to the UK he would then be arrested.

Part III What does the future hold for fathers?

Chapter 14
Recent changes: the impact for fathers

Child Support

The Child Support Agency

The whole area of child maintenance has been through a major shake-up and the Child Support system has been completely reformed. The Government's plans for reform were set out in a White Paper *A new contract for welfare: Children's Rights and Parents Responsibilities* published in July 1999. The Child Support Pensions and Social Security Act became law in July 2000 and sets out the basic structure for the new scheme.

From 3 March 2003 there is a new way of calculating child maintenance. The relevance of child support for the purposes of this book is that it is the non-resident father who pays. Furthermore, the number of days the children stay with their father does have an effect upon the amount of child support he pays, so it is worth a brief overview of the new system.

The road to hell is paved with good intentions – Child Support Act 1991

The intention behind The Child Support Act 1991 was that it would benefit children by ensuring they would receive maintenance from the absent parent, usually their father. The Child Support Agency (CSA) was set up in 1993 and the whole idea was that from then on the agency, rather than the courts, would deal with Child maintenance. There were problems:
- The formula for calculating maintenance was too complicated.
- The Agency was unable to deal with the backlog of claims and reviews of claims because the whole process was cumbersome.

The result of this was:
- Children did not benefit. Statistics show that only one in five children

derived some benefit from the Agency.
- The Act did not deliver what was intended.

The intention behind the 2000 Act was to make the whole area of child maintenance easier to understand, more accessible and easier to enforce so that there is more money for the children.

The new formula

The new system provides that the maintenance a non-resident father pays for any relevant children is calculated as a percentage of his net income. There are four rates of pay.

The rates of pay

- Basic rate: This applies to a non-resident father with a net weekly income of between £200 and £2,000. The percentage of net income is 15% for one child, 20% for two children rising to a maximum of 25% for three children or more. The resident parent can apply to the court for a top-up maintenance order in certain circumstances. For example, where there are additional educational expenses or the child is disabled.
- Reduced rate: This applies to a non-resident father with a net weekly income over £100 but under £200. He will pay £5 per week on the first £100 of his net income and a percentage of his net weekly income over £100. The percentages used to calculate the maintenance are different from the basic rate ones.
- Flat rate: This applies to a non-resident father with a net weekly income of £100 or less, or who is on benefits. The flat rate is £5, irrespective of the number of children.
- Nil rate: This applies to a non-resident father who is any of the following: a full time student; aged 16 to 19 and studying full time for A levels or NVQ level 3; a prisoner; living in a residential home or nursing home and receiving assistance for those costs.

Calculation of net income

What is taken into account and what is not?
- Tax, National Insurance and pension contributions will be deducted from a non-resident father's gross income.
- No deduction is made for a non-resident father's housing costs, even if a large proportion of his income is paid towards those costs!
- If he has investment income that will be included in calculating his net income.
- Deductions are made from the non-resident father's income for relevant 'other' children. A relevant other child includes his natural child from another relationship but the child does not have to be his natural child.

A stepchild is included. It is sufficient that the child is a member of his household and that he or his new partner receives child benefit. The percentage deducted depends upon the number of relevant other children the non-resident father has and whether he pays under the basic rate or reduced rate, as this will alter the percentage to be deducted. The CSA maintenance calculation will be a percentage of what is left of his income after all deductions have been made.

- What about those who appear to have no/a limited income? A non-resident father will be given a deemed income if it can be shown that his lifestyle exceeds his professed income and that he ought to pay higher maintenance. An example would be someone who deals a lot in cash and does not declare his true income.
- The mother's income is ignored under the new formula.
- There are a number of variations that can be made to increase or reduce the maintenance. For example, if a non-resident father pays boarding school fees for the relevant children that would be a ground for a variation.

Shared care

Maintenance is scaled down according to the amount of time the children spend with the non-resident father. The more the children stay with him, the less maintenance he pays as follows:

Number of nights	Fraction to subtract
52 to 103	One-seventh
104 to 155	Two- sevenths
156 to 174	Three-seventh
175 or more	One-half

There might be a situation where the non-resident father has qualifying children to stay for a different number of days. Here he would add up the total number of days for all the children who stay with him and divide by the number of children. For example, if child A stays 104 nights and child B 104 nights the scaling down is 2/7th and 2/7th divided by 2 = 2/14ths.

If the one-half threshold is reached for any given child, that is they stay with him for 175 days or more, then the maintenance is reduced by a further £7.

As indicated above this is a brief overview of the new Child Support formula and not meant to be a definitive guide. The Child Support Agency has produced some useful literature on the implications of the new formula and all this information can be found on their website.

The Human Rights Act 1998

Implications of the Human Rights Act for fathers

The Human Rights Act does not provide more rights for a father, but it should provide easier access to those rights. The Act came into force on 2 October 2000 and incorporates into British law 'most' of the provisions of the European Convention on Human Rights (the Convention). The rights we have implemented are called 'convention rights'. This should not to be confused with the Hague Convention.

If a father makes an application under the Children Act what effect will the Human Rights Act have on the court's decision?

From now on, whenever a UK court is considering the existing law, it will have to look at that law and see whether it fits in with Convention rights. The law must be read in a way compatible with Convention rights, so if the court finds that a particular Act of Parliament does not fit with Convention rights what can the court do?

The court can only make what is called a 'declaration of incompatibility' because the Human Rights Act does not allow the courts to overrule an Act of Parliament. It is only the higher courts that will be able to make declarations of incompatibility, so in a family case if a query arises in the family proceedings court or county court, the case should be transferred to the High Court. The Government and Parliament have to decide if the law should be changed.

The Children Act was drafted with the intention that it would be compatible with the Act. The courts must read and give effect to children legislation in a way which is compatible with the Convention rights, so far as it is possible to do so, and it will be necessary for the courts to evaluate the effect of the legislation in particular cases to ensure compatibility.

It is not explicitly stated in the Convention that the children's interests are the paramount consideration, and the European Court, in interpreting the right to family life, has stated that the rights and freedoms of all concerned must be taken into account and a fair balance struck. The European Court has found that the best interests of a child may be the paramount factor in determining custody. The Commission has also said that the child's interests are dominant if there is conflict between the parent and child, in which event the interests of the child prevail. The European courts have not clearly indicated what factors the domestic courts should take into account in determining what is in the best interests of the child, but have indicated the importance of the continuity of development or consistency in the upbringing of a child.

Can a father bring a claim?

The Human Rights Act is like a code of conduct. This is set down in the form of Articles and Protocols. It is not a series of dos and don'ts. If a father wants to take somebody to court under the Act, he needs to show that the code of conduct has been breached. In legal terms this means he is a person who is a 'victim' of a breach of Convention rights.

Who are victims and how does a victim bring a claim?

A victim is a person. This includes an individual or a company, because in law a company is a legal person. The breach could be due to action taken, or failure to take action. The father need not have suffered harm because of the breach, provided there is a risk of him being directly affected. He could bring a claim if his family is at risk of being broken up by a particular policy, even if this has not occurred; for example, against a local authority that has made an application to take his child into care although the application has not yet been heard in court.

Who can a claim be brought against?

Public authorities alone have a duty to comply with the Convention, not individuals. In a contact case it is not possible for the father to complain that the mother is not respecting his right to family life by denying him the contact he desires. Public authorities include local authorities, the Police, and the Courts to ensure a fair hearing.

Which convention rights are going to affect Family law and fathers' rights?

Article 6: the right to a fair trial

Just because a father does not succeed in his case, it does not mean that he did not have a fair trial – but everybody has a right to a fair trial. Each party must have a reasonable opportunity to present his/her case, including evidence, under conditions that do not place either of them at a disadvantage to the other:

- Cases must be brought within a reasonable time. Delays where cases are not listed for lack of court resources will be unacceptable under the Convention and have been held to be a violation of it, but delays in other European jurisdictions are such that some UK delays may not seem that unreasonable. However, in relation to children, especially where a child has been removed from his/her parents, or contact has been stopped pending the final court hearing, delay is crucial and here there is a very real prospect that Article 6 could be breached.
- There must be an independent judge.

- Everyone is entitled to a public hearing and for the judge's decision to be pronounced in public. However, there are circumstances when a public hearing would not be appropriate, such as cases involving children. The proceedings are in chambers, that is, behind closed doors, and not open court.
- There is a right to know the judge's reasons for the decision.

Article 6 will be broken if these standards have not been met. Article 6 covers criminal and civil proceedings. Civil proceedings that are covered by Article 6 include disputes about with whom the children of separated parents should live, so Article 6 will be relevant in relation to contact disputes.

Article 8: the right to respect for private and family life.

Respect for private life.

There is no firm definition but it covers:
- The right for a person to get on with his own life without interference.
- The right to develop his personality and to form friendships and relationships with other people.
- The right to enjoy his sexuality.
- The right to control his body.

Respect for family life.

This does not allow persons to claim a right to establish family life. It is a question of fact, taking into account all the circumstances. Some examples of family life are as follows:
- A married couple with children. A child born to married parents will be part of that relationship from the moment he/she is born.
- An unmarried father who cohabits with the mother and the children.
- Where the parties do not cohabit but the unmarried father has regular contact with his child and a strong bond, showing that there are family ties. He should show commitment, although where an unmarried father had not had regular contact with his child, family life has been found.
- A single mother and child.
- Family life has been held to exist where there is no blood link or legal link through adoption or marriage.
- Family life goes beyond the traditional family and may be established between children and individuals not necessarily their parents to the extended family life.
- When parents divorce or separate their relationship ceases to be family life within the meaning of Article 8, but the relationship between parent and child may survive as family life. Contact is relevant here.

- It has been held to include a right for parents to insist measures are taken by public authorities to re-unite them with their children. Local authorities run particular risks in relation to contravention of the Convention with regard to children in care. The right of parents to maintain relationships with their children can be violated by termination of contact and placing for adoption.
- The right to information has been considered to be an aspect of family life protected by Article 8 in relation to records kept by a local authority for a child in their care.

What would be a justifiable interference into family life?

Article 8 is not an absolute right but a qualified one. This means that a public authority can break the right in certain circumstances so that it can intervene, but the public authority will have to show that it had a sound legal reason for doing so and that it was reasonable in all the circumstances of the case.

There is a balancing exercise between a court respecting an individual's right to his private life, and welfare of children. In cases where a court declines to make a contact order, particularly in implacable hostility cases, the Court will have to justify the decision that in the interests of the child the refusal was justifiable.

Cultural and religious practises have to be considered carefully as failure to respect them could result in the court and local authorities being in breach. An example of this is a case where the parties were Moroccan. When the parties were together, the whole family slept in the same bed. After separation the father continued to sleep with the children on contact visits in the same bed. A Child Welfare Officer reporting on this case felt that there was something 'suspect' about the behaviour and referred to it in an extremely derogatory way.

Care proceedings 'proper' will invite questions over family life and its disruption. Interference cannot be justified just because another family might simply provide a better home for the child. The aim of care proceedings will usually be to reunite the family as soon as possible.

Article 9: freedom of thought, conscience and religion

The right to bring up children in the religion of their parental choice is usually accepted as a parental right, but this can be a difficult area and it can be complicated. This is particularly so where both parents are of different religions and when they have separated there is a tug of war over the religion of the child. There may be applications within the Children Act.

Article 14: prohibition of discrimination

Parental responsibility is an area where unmarried fathers have been seen as discriminated against. The discrimination has been deemed justified by the court to protect the interests of the child and mother.

Remedies for breach of rights

Changing a decision

If a party wants to change a decision that has been made by a public authority or for the court to order a public authority to do something, or stop doing something, he can apply for a procedure called a judicial review. A judge will review the case and decide if the public authority has acted unlawfully. He has three months from the decision or action he is challenging in which to take this step.

Compensation

If a party wants compensation as a result of a breach of his rights he can bring a claim in damages. He has one year from the date of breach to bring his case.

If his rights have been broken, he may be awarded compensation, but just because there has been a breach of his rights does not mean that he will receive it. It is not clear whether the UK family court has power to award damages. In any event the UK courts will have to take their lead form the European Court in terms of damages.

Declarations of incompatibility

If the courts decide that a particular act does not fit with Convention law, all they can do is to declare it incompatible but they cannot overrule it. Only Parliament can do that.

Chapter 15
Pressure for change

Amendments to the Children Act in respect of parental responsibility

In Chapter 8 we looked at the changes made to this area of the law by The Adoption & Children Act 2002, and the implications for unmarried fathers and stepfathers. In 1998 the Lord Chancellor's Department produced a Consultation Paper *Procedures for the Determination of Paternity and on the Law of Parental Responsibility for Unmarried Fathers* to address these issues. It was considered whether unmarried fathers should be put on an equal footing with married fathers, and be given an automatic right to parental responsibility. The statistics relating to the unmarried family were reviewed.

The paper states that in 1996 there were 649,485 births registered in England and Wales and 232,663 (35.8%) were to unmarried parents. The father's details were included on the birth certificate for 181,647 of these births, that is 78% of them. In 74.4% of these joint registrations – and in 58% of all births outside marriages – the parents were living together. However, in the same year the courts only made 5,587 parental responsibility orders and only around 3,000 parental responsibility agreements are made each year.

The concern was whether parental responsibility as an 'automatic' right should be limited to certain categories of unmarried fathers. Ultimately it was decided to extend the right to unmarried fathers who sign the birth register jointly with the mother and not to extend that right to all unmarried fathers automatically. An unmarried father does not require parental responsibility to apply for residence or contact and so in this respect is not disadvantaged.

We have looked at domestic violence in Chapter 12 and the changes made to the Children Act by the Adoption & Children Act. One of the reasons behind not granting parental responsibility to all unmarried fathers was that such a move could increase the risk of children being exposed to violence from them. There is of course that risk, but then it should be borne in mind that a married father who automatically has parental responsibility could be a violent person and his children be at risk.

Recommendations for contact

There has been ever increasing pressure from relevant legal bodies, interested organizations including fathers' rights groups and individuals to address the issue of post separation contact, to make it work more effectively for fathers and to raise their public profile. If a father shows a genuine commitment to his children and has the capability and capacity to look after them, then his involvement should be encouraged and contact facilitated. The 1998 Consultation Paper *Supporting Families* produced by the Government (and to which we have referred in Chapter 1) stresses the importance of fathers. What can be done for fathers?

Making contact work

A report *Making Contact Work* was published by the Lord Chancellor's Department on 8 February 2002. It addresses:
- The arrangements for contact between children and the parent with whom they do not live and the ways contact can be facilitated. In other words, how both agreements between parents and orders of the court for contact can be best achieved, made to work and sustained over time;
- The other ways contact orders can be enforced. The current law relating specifically to enforcement, by means of committal to prison or fines for breaches of court orders is considered unsatisfactory. We looked at this in Chapter 13; and
- Makes recommendations to the Lord Chancellor about the ways in which contact between children and parents who are undergoing family breakdown can be improved, including the enforcement of contact orders. We look at these below.

Recommendations to the Lord Chancellor

Background

The recommendations in the Report are based upon the responses received from all the relevant legal bodies, representative groups/fathers' interest groups and individuals to the questions posed in a Consultation Paper entitled *Making Contact Work*, and published in March 2001.

The Consultation Paper specifically addressed the basis for contact between separated parents' and their children; the nature of the problem; why contact disputes arise; why they can be so intractable and why their resolution can be so difficult. The Research undertaken for the Consultation Paper confirmed what we have addressed in Part I. They found that where there is a high degree of conflict between the parties, amicable post-separation contact agreements are unrealistic. Even where arrangements are amicable, contact problems are liable to arise due to factors such as the introduction of new partners and changing needs of the children, and a mother's attitude towards a father's role has a bearing upon that role. How other countries approach contact problems was also addressed including methods of enforcement in those countries.

Responses to questions raised

From a father's point of view, the responses received to the questions raised in the Consultation Paper were crucial because they had a direct bearing upon the recommendations made to the Lord Chancellor in the Report. In fact, the preface to the report states that a total of 240 responses were received from all areas of the family justice system, interested bodies and a large number of individual fathers who gave their view of the system and how it had treated them. The responses show that there is a divergence of views in this highly emotive and sensitive area.

What has been highlighted by the report?

- *Dissatisfaction with the current legal system*
  Criticism has come from the judiciary, lawyers, psychiatrists and the parties themselves. Major criticisms include the fact that there is no time at hearings to try to resolve issues, no judicial continuity, too much pressure on the parties and that litigation is counter productive. The CAFCASS report takes too long to prepare. The Report recommends that a CAFCASS officer is present at the first court appointment to attempt in-court conciliation. It is recommended that an officer should spend more time with the children, but CAFCASS needs to be properly funded and structured. As we saw in Chapter 6 this has been recognized and attempts are being made to improve the service offered by CAFCASS.

- *Contact issues need to be addressed by means other than court proceedings*
  The report recommends that there should be additional facilities to enable contact disputes to be resolved by negotiation, conciliation and mediation. Services already in existence should be improved. There should be the provision of information for separating couples about the likely effects of separation, the difficulties they are likely to encounter and the ways in which these difficulties can be addressed. The report states that for 80% of divorcing couples a solicitor is the first port of call.

- *Recognition that the court process will continue to retain a role and that its procedures must be improved to be more effective.*
  An application to the court should be a remedy of last resort, but the

Report recognizes that in intractable cases where there has been abuse or violence or in cases where the parties simply cannot agree arrangements, the court will become involved. Since the court will remain a major feature in determining contact disputes, improvements to procedure is crucial and steps to reduce the adversarial nature of the proceedings need to be taken. The report recognizes that there are an infinite variety of family circumstances and the difficulties of trying to encompass them within the narrow framework of a court order. It recommends that there should be imaginative and creative use of orders for indirect contact where that is appropriate.

- *New legislation relating to enforcement is required to provide the court with a range of remedies in intransigent contact cases where the court order is not being obeyed*
The Report recognizes that the current system is seriously deficient in the means available to enforce its orders and needs changing. It recommends that the court must maintain the power to punish disobedience and that its powers of enforcement must be broadened and facilities must be implemented and so need to be available. It recommends:

- *Non-punitive measures*
This includes Information Meetings or Parenting Programmes for intractable contact disputes or where the offending party is to seek psychiatric advice to deal with the issues.

- *Punitive measures*
Where non-punitive measures have not worked, there could be an order with a penal sanction such as community service or regular attendance at parenting classes. The court could have power to award financial compensation from one parent to another – for example, where the cost of a holiday has been lost. Fines/imprisonment would be used as a last resort and only where there have been flagrant and intentional breaches of court orders without any genuine excuses.

It is recognized that fines and committal to prison are crude and inadequate as a means of addressing the problem of contact orders that have not been implemented. The committal application relating to breach of contact in the first instance should be made without notice to the proposed respondent. It should only proceed if the court took the view that the alleged breach of the order is sufficiently serious for it to warrant committal proceedings going to a full hearing.

What happens now?

The recommendations set out in the Report are helpful, but fathers are dubious as to how much of what is proposed will actually be implemented and when, and whether the proposed methods for enforcement will actually work in practice, that is, if funds are injected to set up the necessary facilities in the first place. Essentially the reform they are looking for is more fundamental than this and relates to their status as the non-resident parent. What they are looking for is a presumption of shared care.

Shared residence

Is this a new concept?

The Children Act actually does provide for shared residence, so this is not a new concept. The report *Making Contact Work* considered the question of joint residence/shared parenting. It was decided that a move towards shared residence at this juncture was not appropriate. It would require 'substantial investigation and validation' and therefore recommendations could not be made for it to be implemented. However, the Report canvassed the possibility of the Government setting up a pilot scheme based on a small number of courts to test the effect of such orders in practice.

How would this help?

Fathers want equal treatment. They feel discriminated against. They do not like the term 'non-resident' parent. Many fathers complain that while the parties were together the mother was more than happy for them to share equally in the child care duties and actively encouraged their relationship with the children, but that as soon as the relationship came to an end the rules were changed.

On the basis that many mothers expect men should share equally in raising their children, it would be thought that these women would support some form of shared parenting arrangement. After all, if children are living with their father some of the time, the mother's time would be freed up enabling her to pursue other interests or even to advance her career if she has/had one.

Although there are mothers who do actively encourage contact and who strive with the father to work together for the benefit of the children, this is not the same as having shared residence. Many fathers feel that the mother assumes she has superior rights to the father because she is the mother and may therefore resist the father's equal involvement. They say it's all about being in control.

What does the Children Act actually say about shared residence?

During the course of its passage through Parliament many amendments were made to the Children Bill and recommendations made to Parliament by all the children organizations, legal bodies and charities, and it is clear that it was originally intended for shared residence orders to be made. House of Commons reference sheet 89/5.13 on the Children Bill (26 June 1989) states:

It is intended that another difference between residence and custody orders is that the new order should be flexible enough to accommodate a much wider range of situations. In some cases, the order will provide that the child shall live with both parents, even though they do not share the same household. If such an arrangement is practicable, there is no reason to discourage it.

More commonly, however, the order will provide that the child shall live with both parents, but to spend more time with one than the other...

It is a more realistic description of the responsibilities involved in arrangements of this sort to make a residence order covering both parents rather than a residence order for one and a contact order for the other.

The Children Act 1989 Guidance and Regulations state that a shared care order has the advantage of being more realistic in those cases where the child is to spend considerable amounts of time with both parents. Furthermore, it removes any impression that one parent is good and responsible whereas the other parent is not. However, the guidelines also state it was not expected that it would become a common form of order! Confused? What does the Children Act say exactly?

Does shared residence mean equal share?

The Children Act states that a residence order may be made in favour of more than one person at the same time even though they do not live together and that it may specify the periods during which the child is to live in the different households concerned. It follows on from this that a shared residence order does not mean that the children will spend half their time with each parent. It could be weekends with one parent and weekdays with the other parent; alternate weeks with each parent or term-time with one parent and holidays with the other, or other arrangements where the child is to spend large amounts of time with each parent.

Why are shared residence orders seldom ever made?

Attitude of the courts

What is the judicial reasoning behind all of this? Traditionally the courts have recognized that in some circumstances a shared residence order can reduce the bitterness between the parties, but it has been stressed that there would have to be unusual circumstances where it would be of positive benefit to the child. The court could make a shared residence order in unusual but not unnecessarily exceptional circumstances. This could be where the child has a settled home with one parent and substantial contact with the other. This type of order can also be used to confer parental responsibility on a stepparent.

A fairly recent Court of Appeal case has held that it is not necessary to demonstrate exceptional circumstances or a positive benefit to the child. It is sufficient to show that the order would be in his interests. This may be appropriate where, for example, there has been shared care for a period of time and during that time the child has coped well with the arrangements.

However, it is not that simple. Almost invariably the circumstances dictate that the child should make a settled home with one parent because two competing homes would lead to confusion and stress. So a joint residence order is not made in conventional situations, as children generally need the stability of a single home. In any event, the decision to make a shared residence order is at the discretion of the court on the specific facts of the particular case.

What do the legal advisors think?

Lawyers tend to follow the case law and as a result few applications for shared residence are made. For many there is no point. A father would just be wasting his time and money because, on balance, he would be unlikely to succeed. Court Welfare Officers have not recommended them in the past and, on the basis that the court gives considerable weight to what a welfare officer recommends, what chance would a father have in succeeding in such an application? What is a father supposed to do?

Why it is so difficult to obtain a shared residence order (apparently)?

The courts have made it clear that if there are issues to be resolved in relation to the amount of contact or educational arrangements an application would fail. Unless all the arrangements are agreed there can be no order. This is very confusing because where arrangements are agreed, the court would not be making an order anyway. It seems once again that a father is in a no-win situation.

Resolving the issue

The pro-father organizations state that if the starting point was that there was a presumption of shared residence, which could only be set aside where there was a strong and clear case for doing so, then at least fathers would not be disadvantaged from the outset. If there was a shared residence order, then the distinction between the resident and non-resident parent would disappear as would a lot of the resentment.

Removing contact and conflict

When mothers have residence fathers feel sidelined and forced to make contact applications and it is soul destroying even if, after months of battling to obtain a contact order, a mother still does not comply to allow the contact to proceed. It is argued that fathers would not need to make repeated applications for contact if a shared residence order was the standard post separation order. In fact, many of the contact problems would fall away. Currently we have contact and conflict.

What do the pro-father groups think?

Organizations acting for fathers are in favour of such orders. Their view is that such orders merely tie in with the original intention of Parliament and the Children Act itself which permits an order for shared residence. In the report *Making Contact Work* it was stated that there were practical objections to shared residence because, although the argument that shared parenting might restrict the scope for disagreements and bitterness was followed, it was doubted whether in practice this would happen. Other practical objections were that:

- Where the parties live a long way away from each other it would be impractical.
- Parents do not always behave rationally and reasonably in the context of parental separation. One parent may need protection from the other and the child the same protection.

Revisiting fatherhood

The decision of the Court of Appeal re: the 'house husband' case (which we looked at in Chapter 11) raised fundamental issues about the merits of fatherhood as opposed to motherhood and a father's contribution to the welfare and needs of his children. As far as fathers are concerned the decision has serious implications because on the face of it, this was a father who had an exceptionally strong case and he still did not succeed in his application. What hope, then, is there for fathers?

Whatever the legal arguments advanced for the decision in the above case, the view of fathers is that it is biased against them and the legal profession as a whole need to address the fact that there is much dissatisfaction with the current law. Many lawyers are of the view that the problem stems from the fact that since cases such as this are held in private and full details are not released to the public, it is no surprise that the decisions are being misinterpreted because the full reasoning behind the decisions is not given to the public. Further, it is argued that the media and the public should be aware that decisions are not made lightly, but only after a detailed analysis of the facts and the law and a consideration of what is in the best interests of the children. Some lawyers say that there should be more openness and that if judgments were given in open court while preserving the anonymity of the parties concerned, then there would not be this misinterpretation of the facts. With respect, that is not actually the essence of the problem.

Time for change

What is the essence of the problem? As far as fathers are concerned this is all about the inherent differences between men and women and more importantly, the perception by the establishment of what their respective roles as parents are within our society. We looked at the family unit and a father's role within it in Chapter 1. The fact is that society has changed, and so has the family unit,, but the establishment's view of fatherhood has not moved forward with it.

The 'economic' view of fatherhood persists. As Counsel for the father in the 'house husband' case pointed out, if it was the father who had given up work then very different considerations would have applied. The stereotypical view of fatherhood needs to change as it is far removed from the realities of modern fatherhood. The profile of fathers and fatherhood needs to be raised and policy makers need to focus on the positive part that loving and devoted fathers have to play as well as look at what can be done to support the role of fathers.

Final thoughts

For fathers it is not a question of taking the children away from their mothers, but about giving loving, caring and responsible fathers a proper chance to be as involved as possible with their children where they are genuinely devoted and committed to them. A court order can never be a substitute for a fair and agreed arrangement between two parents genuinely acting in their child's interests but, on the basis the law will continue to be used to decide what the parents cannot, it is ever more crucial that changes are made.

The representatives for fathers have argued for a very long time that the courts must take into account the impact of decisions on children and fathers and their future relationships and review the approach to the making of, in particular, residence and contact orders under the Children Act.

Fathers do not think that enough lawyers are actually doing anything to press for changes within the law, even though the lawyers know the law they are applying is not working. This is why they are being accused by fathers of making a living out of their misery. It is no longer an acceptable defence for lawyers, and this includes judges who have been heavily criticized, to assert to fathers that they are just applying the law as legislated by Parliament and subsequently construed in the courts.

Appendix

Some useful contacts and addresses

Catholic Marriage Advisory Council
Clitheroe House
1 Blythe Mews
Blythe Road
London W14 0NW
tel (+44) (0) 20 7937 3781

Child Abduction Unit
81 Chancery Lane
London WC2A 1DD
tel (+44) (0) 20 7911 7094/7047
enquiries (+44) (0) 20 7911 7127
fax (+44) (0) 20 7911 7248

Children & Family Court Advisory & Support Service (CAFCASS)
CAFCASS Headquarters
13th and 14th Floors
Archway Tower
2 Junction Road
London N19 5HQ
tel (+44) (0) 20 7210 4400
fax (+44) (0) 20 7210 4422
email cafcass@cafcass.gov.uk

Child Support Agency
There are various offices
tel 08457 133133
email csa-nel@new100.dss.gsi.gov.uk
www.dss.gov.uk/csa
Herald House
tel (+44) (0) 20 79209491

Fathers websites
There are numerous websites for fathers. A couple of websites which contain links to sites for father are:
www.dads-uk.co.uk/resources.htm
www.coeffic.demon.co.uk/organiz.htm

Foreign & Commonwealth Office
Consular Department
Clive House
Petty France
London SW1H 9HD
tel (+44) (0) 20 72704017

International Social Services
39 Brixton Road
London SW9 6DD
(if the child is abducted abroad they can make enquiries about his/her whereabouts)

Jewish Marriage Council
Head Office
23 Ravenshurst Avenue
London NW4 4EE
tel (+44) (0) 20 8203 6311
fax (+44) (0) 20 8203 8727
email jmc@brijnet.org
www.jmc-uk.org

The Law Society
Law Society Hall
113 Chancery Lane
London WC2A 1PL
tel (+44) (0) 20 7242 1222
fax (+44) (0) 20 7831 0344
email info.services@lawsociety.org.uk
www.lawsociety.org.uk

Office for the Supervision of Solicitors
Victoria Court
8 Dormer Place
Royal Leamington Spa
Warwickshire CV32 5AE
tel 0845 608 6565
www.oss.lawsociety.org.uk

Records Centre/Information Services
tel 0870 606 2555
www.solicitors-online.com

Legal Assistance
National Association of Citizens Advice
Bureau (CAB)s
www.nacab.org.uk
www.adviceguide.org.uk
Law Centres Federation
www.lawcentres.org.uk
Federation of Independent Advice
Centres
www.fiac.org.uk

Legal Services Commission
CLS Funding
85 Gray's Inn Road
London WC1X 8TX
tel (+44) (0) 20 7759000
local rate 08456081122
Minicom 0845 609 66
www.justask.org.uk (Guide to online
legal services)

**The National Association of Child
Contact Centres (NACC)**
Minerva House
Spaniel Row
Nottingham NG1 6EP
tel (+44) (0) 115 948 4557
www.nacc.org.uk

National Family Mediation
9 Tavistock Place
London WC1H 9SN
tel (+44) (0) 20 7383 5993
fax (+44) (0) 20 7383 5994
email general@nfm.org.uk
www.nfm.u-net.com

**The National Family and Parenting
Institute**
430 Highgate Studios
53-57 Highgate Road
London NW5 1TL
tel (+44) (0) 20 7424 3460
fax (+44) (0) 20 7485 3590
email info@nfpi.org
www.nfpi.org

NEWPIN
NEWPIN offers specific services for young
and black, ethnic minority fathers.
Amersham Centre
Inville Road
London SE17 2HY
tel (+44) (0) 20 77408997
email
fathers@nationalnewpin.freeserve.co.uk
contact Celestine Chakravarty-Agbo

Principal Registry of the High Court
The Divorce Registry
First Avenue House
42-49 High Holborn
London WC1V 6NP
tel (+44) (0) 20 79476000

Reunite
National Council for Abducted Children
PO Box 158
London N4 1AU
tel (+44) (0) 20 7404 8356
and
PO Box 113
Leicester LE2 0EF
tel (+44) (0) 1533 624460

Royal Courts of Justice (High Court)
Strand
London WC2
tel (+44) (0) 20 79476000

The Solicitors Family Law Association
PO Box 302
Orpington
Kent BR6 8QX
tel (+44) (0) 1689 850 227
fax (+44) (0) 1689 855 833

**UK College of Family Mediators
(UKCFM)**
24-32 Stephenson Way
London NW1 2HX
tel (+44) (0) 20 7391 9162
fax (+44) (0) 20 7391 9165
email info@ukcfm.co.uk
www.ukcfm.co.uk